YORK FILM NOTES

Citizen Kane

Director
Orson Welles

Note by Dan Williams

D0271099

Longman   York Press

York Press
322 Old Brompton Road, London SW5 9JH

Pearson Education Limited
Edinburgh Gate, Harlow, Essex CM20 2JE, United Kingdom
Associated companies, branches and representatives throughout
the world

First published 2000

ISBN 0-582-40493-2

Designed by Vicki Pacey
Phototypeset by Gem Graphics, Trenance, Mawgan Porth, Cornwall
Colour reproduction and film output by Spectrum Colour
Printed in Malaysia, KVP

contents

background 5

trailer 5
reading citizen kane 6
■ the greatest film? 6
■ kane and hearst 9
■ rosebud 11
key players' biographies 11
director as auteur 20

narrative & form 23

themes 23
■ the opening 24
■ cause and effect 29
characterisation 32
chronology & temporal order 36
equilibrium & disequilibrium 39

style 44

mise-en-scène 44
■ deep focus 44
■ space & filming 45
■ setting, décor, costume & make-up 49
■ lighting 51
montage 55
the soundtrack 58

contexts 62

Ideology 62
■ gender in citizen kane 65
production history 67
■ industrial context 73
cultural contexts 75
■ filmography 78
■ genre 79
■ summary 81
the audience 82
critical responses 84
conclusion 87

bibliography 88
cinematic terms 91
credits 93

author of this note Dan Williams teaches Film Studies at the Department of Continuing Education, City University, London. Having completed an MA in Film Studies at the University of East Anglia, he has, since 1990, taught Film Studies in adult and higher education. He contributed two entries – *Paris, Texas* and *My Beautiful Launderette* – to the *International Dictionary of Films and Filmmaking*.

background

trailer *p5*   **reading Citizen Kane** *p6*   **key players' biographies** *p11*
director as auteur *p20*

trailer

When *Citizen Kane* was released in 1941 it was instantly recognised by many critics as a classic. However reactions were mixed and some reviewers were critical:

> *Citizen Kane* is far and away the most surprising and cinematically exciting motion picture to be seen here in many a moon. As a matter of fact it comes close to being the most sensational film ever made in Hollywood.
>
> *Bosley Crowther, New York Times, 2 May 1941*

> As for *Citizen Kane*, wicked, exhausting, satirical, clever *Citizen Kane*, experiment in new camera angles as it is, I must see it again, for each time I find something that I missed before. But it's no film for relaxation. Its author-actor-director Orson Welles is a man apart.
>
> *Evelyn Russell, Sight and Sound, Spring 1942*

> Its style is essentially theatrical but is unusual in its narrative construction, in its dialogue, which has been written with amazing realism (as where a single voice rises out of a babble of voices and suddenly dominates the rest) and above all in its pictorial composition.
>
> *Monthly Film Bulletin, December 1941*

The following review in a magazine for film exhibitors carried the headline:

> *Citizen Kane*. Outstanding Achievement in Film History.
> The story of a newspaper genius, an egotist who had everything the world had to offer, it compels attention and admiration

through its vital camera work, scarifying dialogue, blunt realism, freedom from sentimentality, unique technical treatment and flawless portrayals.

News and Property Gazette 'Today's Cinema', 7 October 1941

The more critical reviews included this one:

Citizen Kane, for all its laudable attempt to blaze a new trail in the cinematic forest, is a disconcerting mixture of cold virtuosity and empty pyrotechnics.

Herman G. Weinberg, Sight and Sound, Spring 1941

reading citizen kane

THE GREATEST FILM?

Since its initial release, *Citizen Kane* has frequently been described as the greatest film ever made. In 1961–2 a survey of critics, organised by *Sight and Sound*, placed the film at Number One. This position was repeated in succeeding polls carried out by the magazine. In 1998 the film was voted Number One in the American Film Institute's Top 100 films.

Looking at the film now, we will:

■ Consider whether this reputation is valid

■ See how *Citizen Kane* is significant as an original, artistic creation

■ Discuss how the film relates to the style of film-making developed by Hollywood studios up to 1941, and the influence of European expressionistic lighting and montage editing

■ Consider the film in relation to events outside the film industry. Orson Welles directed the film when he was just twenty-five years old and relevant information about his life, and other people who made the film, provides a perspective on its creation

■ Consider how the film relates to prevailing ideas within American society in 1941, and the influence of economic and cultural factors

■ *Citizen Kane* became more critically respected after its initial release, so

reading citizen kane

it is also relevant to see how the film relates to ideas about film-making which have developed since 1941

■ This account of the film aims to show why it has been consistently described as a 'masterpiece' and why many film critics have been inspired to write and talk about this film in such extreme terms.

Kane is a figure who holds our attention. The story of his life is full of drama, humour and melodramatic emotions, all presented in a way that shows a mastering of the formal techniques involved in cinema. He is a powerful personality whose true identity remains elusive and, because there is a sense in which he experiences the loss of a meaningful world, he has been compared with the alienated protagonists of modernist fiction. Various critics have also talked about an emptiness at the centre of his character.

The film has also been celebrated as a work of art because it develops imaginative themes while at the same time exploring familiar ones from other works, such as the transition made by a character from a lower-class background to extreme wealth.

The film presents a startling opening sequence in which the main character dies. Right from the outset the action is unusual in relation to Hollywood conventions because most films made by the industry rely on building a strong identification with a hero or heroine. The early death of Kane threatens this process. The audience is confronted with the situation of Kane's death and an enigmatic representation of the final moments before he dies. Nevertheless the film goes on to create dramatic tension in the account of Kane's life.

Following the presentation of a newsreel report, narrative involvement is developed through a series of flashbacks prompted by the memories of friends and acquaintances as the reporter seeks to find out what Kane meant by his final word, 'rosebud'. This enigmatic word proves elusive for the reporter, but he gathers sufficient information for a detailed psychological portrait of Kane to emerge, which allows a wider appreciation and understanding of the incidents and dramatic shifts in his life.

complex nature of his personality

We find that despite Kane's enormous wealth and power there was an underlying sense of unhappiness in his life. He dies alone, uncared for by friends and family. His initial acquisition of wealth was due to circumstances beyond his own free will, revealed by the *News on the March* sequence. Kane's fortune was acquired when a lodger at Mrs Kane's boarding house failed to pay his rent but left instead the rights to a fortune based on ownership of the Colorado goldmine. Mrs Kane's explains her decision to have this fortune passed on to her son and used for his education as a means of protecting him from her husband.

The film suggests that the extreme wealth which Kane acquires does not necessarily bring happiness. This does not mean that the film challenges the truth or values embodied in the so-called American dream – that everyone is free to achieve happiness through the pursuit of wealth. Kane's situation is presented as unique and extreme. The story concentrates on the complex nature of his personality. He becomes a tyrant, but we also feel some sympathy for him. Finally the audience is placed in a privileged position as we see that 'rosebud' referred to his childhood sledge, which is thrown on a fire.

Citizen Kane brings together different approaches to film form. The narrative structure in which the main character dies and his life is recounted in flashback, draws on the example of *The Power and the Glory*, made in 1933 from a Preston Sturges script which has a similar narrative structure.

After the shock of the opening sequences *Citizen Kane* depicts, like many other films, the rise of a central protagonist as Kane succeeds with *The Inquirer*, the newspaper which he owns. And yet we see the influence of the ancient genre of tragedy as this character fails to achieve his aims due to fatal weaknesses.

The story of Kane's life has a dynamic momentum with dramatic narrative developments, yet we are informed about many details of his life as well as his death in the newsreel used after the first sequence. This provides the quality of audience fore-knowledge present in classical tragedy.

The sense of tragedy is increased by the expressive power of different approaches to film style. For example, the widely acclaimed performance by Orson Welles conveys the spirit of a man who progressively loses touch with the world around him and with his second wife Susan. Towards the end, the sinister, Gothic sets of Xanadu convey the loneliness experienced by Susan and by Kane himself. They demonstrate the enormous wealth that has been acquired but also the distance between Kane's life and normality.

There is a much stronger sense of ambiguity in this drama than in many preceding Hollywood films, so the film leaves scope for the viewer's imagination as different interpretations of what the story means become possible. Later in this section we will consider the relevance of biographical information about the makers of the film as a context for understanding *Citizen Kane* and the '**auteur** theory' as one critical approach which can be used to interpret it.

In Narrative and Form we will see how the film's form is constructed through an approach to narrative found in **classical Hollywood** cinema, but also how originality is achieved through, for instance, a distinctive use of flashbacks.

In Style we will see how the style of the film contributes to the narrative, shows a strong concern with creating a sense of '**realism**', and also how unusual expressive effects are created increasing the possibility for different interpretations of the story.

In Contexts the film will be considered more fully in relation to relevant historical contexts including discussion of 'ideology', a concept which can be used to inform historical analysis.

Firstly, however, we will look briefly at two of the main reasons why the film initially attracted critical attention: the relationship of the film to William Randolph Hearst and the mystique around 'rosebud'.

KANE AND HEARST

The film was controversial because the character of Kane was apparently modelled on William Randolph Hearst, a newspaper tycoon still alive at the time. Orson Welles denied that there was a direct connection, arguing that the central character was inspired by a range of tycoon figures in history. For Welles, in other words, Kane is a typical media baron operating in the first half of the twentieth century and, as such, draws on the lives of various powerful individuals.

Controversy and debate about how far Hearst is represented has continued since and there are a number of strong points of comparison between Hearst and Kane. Hearst was a powerful newspaper magnate who inherited a fortune based on mining, and whose success depended on a new sensationalist style of journalism. Although he was a member of the House of Representatives from 1903–1907 Hearst experienced failure in politics, unsuccessfully standing to be mayor of New York. Kane's lack of success as an election candidate and his use of the newspaper in relation to political aims provides a provocative parallel with these events.

When Kane marries his second wife, Susan Alexander, she is portrayed as a failing opera singer, driven to the point of suicide by his ruthless ambition that she should succeed. At one level, Hearst's life offers some comparisons with this relationship. He lived with his partner, Marion Davies, in a luxury palace similar to Kane's fantasy castle Xanadu. Hearst promoted Davies's career as a film star, but the latter was clearly successful and did not suffer the humiliation endured by Susan in the film. Also Hearst and Davies remained a couple, whereas Kane and Susan separate painfully when she decides to leave him.

Other points of similarity and divergence between the life of Kane and Hearst mean that it is difficult to know just how far viewers at the time would have seen the film as a satire. The screen-writer Herman Mankiewicz, who is given a joint credit with Orson Welles, had socialised with Hearst and Davies, and his writing appears to draw on this experience.

The fact that Orson Welles denies the connection may be partly explained by his intention to save the film from legal action. Nevertheless it remains true that the character is far more than just a copy of Hearst. Some critics have argued that this portrait of a powerful but ultimately unhappy public figure bears similarities to Orson Welles himself.

As a fictional creation the character is open to different interpretations. Welles was interested in the theme of greatness and the tragic flaws which undermine this, and was influenced by his interest in Shakespeare's work which was developed through his experience in the theatre (see Key Players' Biographies). In the analysis of narrative, characterisation, and style, we will consider Kane as a multi-faceted fictional creation.

failure to overcome conflict

ROSEBUD

So how important is the information about 'rosebud'? At one level Charles Foster Kane's last words remain enigmatic. We do not know why he was thinking back to his childhood sledge or what this meant to him. Since the sledge is shown during the scene where he is taken away from home, it evokes the loss of childhood and draws attention to the way Kane's life was directed by the business world represented by Walter P. Thatcher. Kane becomes a more humane figure because we are reminded of this loss.

At another level 'rosebud' is a more troubling symbol. The sledge reminds us of the conflict which Kane experienced as a boy, but added to this is the association of 'rosebud' with Susan Alexander who Kane treated tyrannically. Kane is shown saying 'rosebud' twice in the film. On both occasions he holds the paperweight which was originally Susan's possession (it can be seen in the background when Kane visits her apartment).

The tranquil world represented by the paperweight's snow scene contrasts with the harsh realities suggested by the representation of Kane's childhood and his relationship with Susan. Having destroyed many objects in a fit of rage following Susan's decision to leave him, Kane holds on to the paperweight and says 'rosebud'. Here a tear comes to his eye emphasising his feeling of loss.

When Kane drops the paperweight prior to his death the action is mysterious. Following the end of the film we can interpret this moment as encapsulating his failure to overcome the conflict in his life which started in childhood and which he failed to resolve through his relationship with Susan. The word 'rosebud' can be related, then, to disturbing aspects of Kane's life but, in itself, the sledge refers directly to Charles Foster Kane's innocence as a child.

key players' biographies

GEORGE ORSON WELLES

He was born in 1915 in Kenosha, Wisconsin. His mother Beatrice pursued a strong interest in women's rights, opera, classical music and the arts. She encouraged her son's interest in high culture at a very early age. His father Richard, who later became alcoholic, was a minor inventor.

The family moved to Chicago three years after Orson's birth. His older brother Richard was diagnosed as schizophrenic at the age of twenty-six, and sent to a mental hospital. Orson Welles's family background can be explored for the sources of conflict expressed in many of his films, while it also provides some explanation for his talents and his personal problems.

Orson was given favourable attention in comparison with his brother. He was pushed hard to practise artistic talents at an early age by his mother, while through his father he must have gained some insight into an irresponsible father-figure as the latter developed a lifestyle involving heavy drinking, gambling and prostitutes. Orson's mother died when he was nine and his father died seven years later.

Citizen Kane's portrait of a boy torn away from his parents establishes an association between Orson Welles and Kane. Another point of similarity is that as a boy Welles had a guardian figure, named Dr Bernstein, a friend of his mother who took a very active role in encouraging the young Welles's artistic talents.

It is significant for *Citizen Kane* that Orson Welles grew up with such a strong sense of himself as an individual. Biographers (such as David Thomson and Simon Callow) discuss both his prodigious talents and his self-centredness, qualities which are shared by Kane.

Welles's personal life as an adult can be seen as a more direct influence on *Citizen Kane*. The fact that Kane separates from his wife can be compared to Welles's divorce from his wife Virginia which occurred before the film was made. He had to pay alimony on the grounds of mental cruelty and was separated from both his wife and young daughter. Certainly the experience of his marriage collapsing must have affected his performance as Kane.

Orson Welles's creative gifts had developed through attendance at a school which provided good opportunities for exploring theatrical talent. He gained experience of different theatrical techniques, such as lighting and directing, and acted in a range of productions.

Before *Citizen Kane* was made he had established himself in theatre and radio. After an acting début in Ireland, at the age of sixteen, he appeared on Broadway at nineteen and was soon working for the Federal Theatre Project. This included work for the Negro Theatre Project for whom Welles directed a version of *Macbeth* set in Haiti. The Federal Theatre Project was government funded, and Orson Welles provided work as a director and as a writer producing a number of adaptations from classic works.

The significance for *Citizen Kane* lies partly in the involvement with culture that was set up with a progressive political purpose. This is a political film, but it is not as clearly left-wing as Orson's final production in 1937 at the Federal Theatre Project. Due to its depiction of workers on strike, this play called *The Cradle Will Rock* was stopped for a while by the authorities.

The commercial nature of Hollywood production is one explanation for the ambiguous political position of *Citizen Kane*. Also Welles made it clear that his political views were not revolutionary but closer to the social democratic reformism of the Roosevelt government. Nevertheless, the basis in political theatre provides some explanation for the satirical attack on power and privilege which *Citizen Kane* provides.

After Welles and John Houseman, the director of the Federal Theatre Project, had arranged for *The Cradle Will Rock* to take place despite the authorities attempts to stop it, Welles resigned and Houseman was dismissed. Both men were clearly interested in progressive politics and the freedom of artistic expression.

Following their departure from the Federal Theatre Project they set up their own company, Mercury, which provided productions which were both experimental and popular. Work here included a version of Shakespeare's *Julius Caesar* which attacked Fascism.

Welles had already established himself in radio. For instance, he had starred in a radio version of *The March of Time* newsreel which involved actors playing out dramas from current affairs. Welles acted in this weekly programme in 1935 and continued with it until 1939. He also adapted literary classics for the radio and in 1938, with the Mercury Theatre Group which included Houseman, started to provide regular material for radio. Their first shows were dominated by Welles who was director, producer, writer and actor for the *First Person Singular* series which involved adaptations of famous literary works.

The power of radio to create a confusion between fact and fiction was shown very dramatically with the Mercury production of H.G. Wells's *War of the Worlds*. Here Orson Welles's voice set off a mass panic as listeners in New Jersey, who had tuned in from a different station during the middle of the programme, believed the broadcaster's message that Martians had invaded their country.

The broadcast had been scripted by a writer called Howard Koch with involvement from Welles and Houseman. The latter suggested interspersing the production with fictional newscasts. The *War of the Worlds'* episode shows how powerfully convincing a media production can be within a specific context. The show increased Orson Welles's status as a celebrity and provided a strong explanation for the belief at R.K.O. that Orson Welles was capable of outstanding success.

The stir caused by this radio broadcast may have influenced Welles's decision to make a controversial film in which the boundaries between fact and fiction are obscured, as they are in *Citizen Kane* with the resemblance between Kane's life and that of William Randolph Hearst.

Less than a year after the shock of *War of the Worlds*, in 1939, at the age of twenty-four, Orson Welles was signed by R.K.O. who had a history of drawing on radio talent. He was given an unusual contract which allowed him freedom to produce, direct, write and act in a feature film. The contract was also extended to include freedom for Welles to work with the Mercury company.

The idea for *Citizen Kane*, however, only developed after Welles's initial plan to make a film of *Heart of Darkness* had been abandoned due to an escalating budget. He was already trying out an idea for a thriller when a meeting with the experienced screenwriter Herman Mankiewicz produced the ideas for *Citizen Kane*.

Both men discussed the idea of a film based on a great but tragic figure. As Simon Callow points out, Welles had been interested in this idea for a long time but Mankiewicz brought in his own ideas during the script-writing process.

In his biography of Welles, David Thomson draws attention to good reasons for thinking that when Mankiewicz wrote the first-version script, he used both Welles and Hearst as models for the character of Kane. The suggestion is that Mankiewicz would have been helped with this by Houseman who knew Welles from their experience of working together.

The scene where Kane has a tantrum and destroys the bedroom furniture is said to have been inspired by a fit, which Welles had during a meeting prior to the production of Kane, in which he threw things at Houseman. Despite many instances of egocentric behaviour in his career, Orson Welles emerges as a sympathetic figure – partly because of recurring conflicts with the Hollywood film industry over control of his films.

Welles's subsequent career as a director did not produce commercial successes or achieve the critical acclaim amassed by *Citizen Kane*. He went on to a wide range of work as film director and actor, as well as continuing in theatre, radio and television.

Films directed by Orson Welles which have received great critical acclaim include *The Magnificent Ambersons* released in 1942, and *Touch of Evil* released in 1958.

His acting career includes other roles, such as Harry Lime in *The Third Man*, which explore the complex psychology of immoral villains. However, Kane did not put Orson Welles's image in a straitjacket. His work extends a long way beyond specialisation in disturbing tragic roles. Orson Welles was drawn to popular entertainment as well as high culture, yet his work suggests someone who did not fit altogether neatly into commercial American film culture.

GREGG TOLAND – PHOTOGRAPHER

Despite the significance of Orson Welles's creative control, *Citizen Kane* resulted from a variety of inspired creative contributions and collaboration.

Gregg Toland, the photographer, described his work as an interpretation of the director's vision. Nevertheless, Gregg Toland's approach to cinematography had a unique impact on the film. When *Citizen Kane* was made he had already established a reputation as one of the most critically respected cameramen in Hollywood. We must also take into account here that although Toland's reputation had certainly arisen because of his own talents, he had also developed approaches to cinematography which other cameramen were exploring.

Throughout his career Gregg Toland worked in Hollywood, gaining respect for his meticulous approach and his professionalism. His ability to contribute new technological ideas was shown early in his career when, with George Barnes, he helped to pioneer a new camera which could be moved while remaining soundproof.

In the 1930s working for Sam Goldwyn Productions, outside the major Hollywood studios, Toland was given freedom to experiment and innovate with new approaches to cinematography. Goldwyn allowed Toland to carry out his own research and experiments into cinematography, supported by his own team of assistants.

Before 1941 Toland's work showed some of the distinctive **deep focus** approach to cinematography found in *Citizen Kane*. As David Bordwell points out, in the late 1930s the films which Toland worked on involved not just the use of deep focus which was present in other films at the time, but also several planes of action in focus, a tendency to use low-key lighting and an emphasis on 'an exaggeratedly, enlarged foreground plane' (David Bordwell in David Bordwell, Janet Staiger, Kristin Thompson, *The Classical Hollywood Cinema*, p. 347). This style is used in *Citizen Kane* where several important shots involve a striking contrast between looming foreground details and action which is in focus on another plane.

Gregg Toland won an academy award for his work on *Wuthering Heights* in 1939. Again comparison can be made with *Citizen Kane* since the use of depth makes a critical contribution to the meaning of the story. However, as David Bordwell points out, *Wuthering Heights* still involves some shots in which 'one or another is out of focus' (*The Classical Hollywood Cinema*, p. 346).

Attracted by the idea of working with a first-time director, Gregg Toland approached Orson Welles. He then, during the production of the film, educated Welles about cinematography and developed further his own interest in creating a style that was as 'realistic' as possible. The two men enjoyed working together and it is difficult to separate who was responsible for particular ideas, but Orson Welles's respect for Gregg Toland is shown by the fact that the latter's name was featured on the credits next to the director. This acknowledgement of Toland's creative role, which John Ford had initiated when they worked together, provides a contrast with other Hollywood films where the cinematographer is not given such a prominent acknowledgement. *Citizen Kane* extended Toland's reputation. In this film Toland used powerful lights, super xx filmstock and introduced a new refined lens coating.

Gregg Toland went on to gain an Oscar for the photography in *The Best Years of Our Lives*, directed by William Wyler.

THE SPECIAL EFFECTS UNIT

At R.K.O., this was run by Vernon Walker, an experienced cameraman who worked there through the 1930s on films such as *Flying Down to Rio*. Despite the importance of Toland's work the Special Effects Unit, which included 'the brilliant innovator Linwood Dunn, pioneer of optical printing' (Simon Callow, *Orson Welles: The Road To Xanadu*, pp. 521–2), also played a very important role in creating many of the unusual shots in *Citizen Kane* relying on such methods as the use of mattes and optical printing. David Bordwell has shown how the Special Effects Department was responsible for some of the deep-focus effects in the film through post-production work.

HERMAN J. MANKIEWICZ – SCREEN-WRITER

Mankiewicz had first become involved in Hollywood film production as a screen-writer following his career as a journalist. From 1922–25 he was drama editor of the *New York Times*, an experience which contributed one idea for *Citizen Kane* since he was almost sacked after producing a negative review. This must have inspired the writing of the scene in which Leland is eventually fired for his negative review of Susan Alexander's performance. Mankiewicz's journalistic experience contributes to the subject and style of *Citizen Kane*. As Ronald Bowers points out, before 1941 Herman Mankiewicz had written a number of screenplays on 'the reporter/ newspaper theme' (Ronald Bowers in *International Dictionary of Films and Filmmaking – 4*, pp. 528–30).

haunting and powerful soundtracks

The sharp, evocative dialogue produced by the characters in *Citizen Kane* drew on Herman Mankiewicz's established skill as a witty, ironic writer. He had no illusions about his craft, stating on one occasion: 'You don't really need to be a writer to write for pictures in the accepted sense of the word. Some of the best scenario writers in Hollywood can't write at all. They simply have a flair for ideas, for situations' (Ronald Bowers in *International Dictionary of Films and Filmmaking – 4*, p. 530). His involvement in comedy had extended to producing films for the Marx Brothers.

By the time he met Orson Welles, Herman Mankiewicz's career had declined and he suffered from alcoholism. From a biographical perspective, the screenplay of *Citizen Kane* can be related to Mankiewicz's experience of failure, his time spent with Hearst and Marion Davies at San Simeon, and possibly to his own conflicts with an authoritarian father.

It has also been pointed out by Richard Merryman that as a child Herman Mankiewicz had a bicycle which he called 'rosebud'. Mankiewicz's experience of writing for major studios, and his experience of writing dialogue as sound cinema emerged during the 1930s, were vital to the final effects achieved in *Citizen Kane*.

In 1973 Pauline Kael argued that Mankiewicz's role in the film had been neglected (see Contexts: Critical responses). Certainly the screen-writer had to struggle with Welles for his joint credit, and when an Oscar was granted for the screenplay neither Welles nor Mankiewicz attended the ceremony.

BERNARD HERRMANN – COMPOSER

Herrmann worked with the Mercury company on radio before making his film début with the score for *Citizen Kane*. His distinctive approach involved using unusual instruments, such as low winds and the vibraphone. His musical composition was also distinctive in the use of 'unresolved chords' which create suspense but also have been interpreted as creating 'a brooding sense of time suspended' (Joseph Milicia in *International Dictionary of Films and Filmmaking – 4*, pp. 376–9).

Herrmann's career in cinema involved haunting and powerful soundtracks in some key Hitchcock films of the 1950s and 1960s. The continued relevance of his powerful moody music to film-making, since the breakdown of the Hollywood studio system, is shown by Scorcese's use of Herrmann's scores in *Taxi Driver*, and the remake of *Cape Fear*.

OTHER SIGNIFICANT CONTRIBUTIONS

In particular, it should be noted that Welles had assembled a group of actors and actresses who he had worked with before on productions ranging from serious drama to popular entertainment. From this group Joseph Cotten and Agnes Moorhead gained the most recognition and fame in their subsequent careers.

Cotten's performance as Leland compares with various roles in his subsequent films, as a character who falls just short of being the hero. A more disturbing form of ambiguity emerged in Cotten's performance as the murdering uncle in Hitchcock's *Shadow of a Doubt*, while his most famous role as a man of integrity occurred opposite Orson Welles in *The Third Man*.

Agnes Moorehead has a small but very significant part as Kane's mother. She was given a more detailed part in *The Magnificent Ambersons* as Aunt Fanny, a role which included a powerful scene of hysteria.

Other members of the cast, such as William Alland, George Couloris, Erskine Sandford, Everett Sloane, Ruth Warrick, Ray Collings, and Paul Stewart, were experienced in radio and in working under Welles's direction. One member of the cast, Dorothy Comingmore, who had already played small parts in feature films, was taken on as Susan after an impressive screen test.

Robert Wise, the editor who worked with Welles on the production, went on to direct a successful R.K.O horror film *The Curse of the Cat People* in 1944, *The Sound of Music* and *West Side Story*.

John Houseman did not have an official role on the film and was therefore uncredited. He subsequently developed a successful career as Hollywood producer.

SUMMARY

This biographical information has concentrated on career details and possible points for contrast and comparison with the contributions made to *Citizen Kane*. Despite Orson Welles's significance, the film also resulted from the collaboration, teamwork and the individual contributions of employees who had, for the most part, gained some experience at the studio, with Mercury or working in the American film industry.

The two recent biographies of Orson Welles by Simon Callow and David Thomson (see Bibliography) provide the information summarised here and a great deal more. Thomson's book also develops extended critical analysis of Welles's films in relation to his life.

Film theory has frequently involved less emphasis on biographical explanation for films. Even the auteur theory, which we will consider next, has often placed a significant emphasis on evidence within the film text itself.

director as auteur

The concept of the **auteur** was developed by writers for the French film journal *Cahiers du Cinema* in the 1950s and 1960s.

The concept was used to make claims of artistic significance for particular films, placing emphasis on the creative role of the director. Orson Welles was one of the directors championed in the *Cahiers du Cinema* journal. For example, Andre Bazin wrote about the enhanced **'realism'** of Orson Welles's films.

Another example of the critical approach, which uses the auteur theory, can be seen in Peter Cowie's book on Orson Welles's films, published in 1973, where in the conclusion Cowie argues that Orson Welles's style can be seen across the different films which he has made. He emphasises the imagination of Welles's work, draws attention to recurring aspects of style, such as camera movement, and themes which are repeated in different films, such as 'ambition, jealousy, egotism and retribution' (Peter Cowie, *The Cinema of Orson Welles*, pp. 217–19).

Applying the auteur theory to *Citizen Kane*, it can be argued that the film shares the theme of the troubled individual protagonist that features in other films directed by Welles. This approach to the main character is familiar from classical tragedy and modernist literature, but Welles moves concern with this type of individual into new scenarios with a distinctive cinematic style.

The style in *Citizen Kane,* and other films, involves the repeated use of such devices as voice-over, deep focus, montage, the long take, expressionistic acting and lighting. These are all used by some other film-makers, which means that in order to understand Welles as an auteur, his use of this style must be understood in relation to the themes which are expressed – such as ambition, the isolation of the individual or a tragic irresolvable conflict between different views on reality.

With his strange decision to put his money into Xanadu, Kane, for instance, shows a different view from the rest of the world. His conflicts with his friend Leland, his wives, and Walter P. Thatcher are echoed by some of the conflicts experienced by George, the central protagonist in Welles's next film, *The Magnificent Ambersons.* (See Filmography for contrast and comparison of *Citizen Kane* with *Touch of Evil.*)

The auteur theory led some critics to suggest that any film made by an auteur should be regarded as more artistic than a film made by a director without this critical status. This approach can lead to weak films being given too much critical praise just because they were made by an auteur. Bazin stood out against this when he argued that although *Citizen Kane* was a masterpiece Welles's later film *Confidential Report* was significantly weaker (André Bazin, 'On the politique des auteurs' in Jim Hillier (ed) *Cahiers du Cinema: The 1950s Neo Realism, Hollywood, New Wave,* pp. 248–53).

While the auteur theory takes account of differences between films, it aims to draw out points of comparison in a director's work and various criticisms of this approach to film analysis can be made. The theory, by placing so much stress on the creativity of the director, does not take sufficient account of different people involved in the production of the film. As previously stated, it can lead to emphasis on the director's originality, at the expense of recognising how the film is part of a tradition, or how it draws on a wide range of influences.

Critical approaches developed since the auteur theory have placed more emphasis on analysing a film in relation to narrative structure and film form, and how the film relates to a historical context – including beliefs within the society and the economic and industrial conditions under which the movie is made.

More recent academic approaches to film have been less interested in critical evaluation of films solely on the basis of the director's role, and more concerned with the role of the film spectator, considering how he/she makes sense of the film. This brings a greater emphasis on understanding how a particular narrative, such as *Citizen Kane*, relates to typical narrative structures in Hollywood cinema, other types of film-making and story-telling in general.

This does not ignore the creative role of individuals, such as the director, but there is certainly more emphasis on how conventions of narrative and film form are used to create meaning.

narrative & form

themes *p23*   characterisation *p32*   chronology and temporal order *p36*
equilibrium and disequilibrium *p39*

themes

The term narrative is used to signify the importance of structure and form, so we are concerned not only with the imaginative content of the film but also how it has been organised. To an extent, the film inevitably fits in with established ways of story-telling found in other Hollywood films. In considering themes, we will:

■ Discover how far *Citizen Kane* conforms with typical approaches to story-telling in classical Hollywood cinema and how the film breaks with these approaches.

■ See how ideas are communicated to the audience through the manipulation of different narrative systems and formal devices.

The film follows a number of themes to develop a complex portrait of Kane as a powerful figure who is flawed by weaknesses of character. Listed below are themes which contribute to this portrait:

1. Charles Foster Kane's adult life involves a loss of integrity. After signing a Declaration of Principles for *The Inquirer*, which involves a commitment to honest reporting, he seems to use the newspaper later to promote his wife's career.

   He sacks his friend Leland after the latter has started a negative review of Susan's performance. Although Kane completes the critical review, it is strongly suggested that Leland is sacked because he failed to comply with the views which Kane wanted him to express.

2. Kane's egotism is related to a tragic inability to feel love. This criticism is provided by Leland and also emerges in Susan's antagonism to Kane.

3. Kane's wealth is extreme. This is established in the newsreel and returned to with Kane's accumulation of possessions (including

artworks from Europe) and the extravagance of Xanadu shown at the end of the film. The ostentatious display of wealth is symptomatic of his greed and the collection of objects is presented as obsessive. Xanadu also represents an escape from a world where he has suffered defeats. For Susan it is like a prison.

4. Kane's loss of childhood is represented by the sledge. The fact that the reporters are unaware of this extends the sense of lost innocence to a wider context. The film also shows how other characters change with age. For instance, Leland and Susan are more knowing as, after the death, they reflect on the meaning of Kane's life.

5. There is a concern with the relationship between Kane's private and public life. The newsreel shows how these two sides to his character are related, but the rest of the film develops our awareness of his personality. There is a strong sense that Kane succeeded in imposing his personality on the public world. However, the film as a whole shows that aspects of his character were hidden from the world at large.

The first shot and the penultimate shot which depict the 'No Trespassing' sign make it clear that ultimately Kane sought to separate himself from the outside world.

6. Finally, there is the enigmatic nature of Kane's personality. The reporter, Thompson, learns a great deal but gaps remain and in the end he concludes there is a missing element.

THE OPENING

The opening sequence provides a prologue to the story. Kane's luxurious palace and his death are presented in a way that is atmospheric. The first image of the fence with the 'No Trespassing' sign immediately conveys that this is a story which explores some kind of conflict. This image, which is repeated at the end of the film, introduces the theme of a division between Kane's private world and his public persona. It is also powerfully enigmatic, simultaneously evoking the idea of Kane as a figure whose emotions are hidden, and that this narrative will involve a tension between what we know and forbidden knowledge.

At the start and end of the film
Xanadu is presented as a haunting
castle in the background, with the
emblem K looming in the foreground
of the image

images of extreme wealth

The palace looks menacing and the details of the location convey a sense of decay, even a sense of nightmare. The strangeness of the action is developed by the lack of information. A light suddenly goes off when we move close to Kane's window. In retrospect this can be interpreted as signifying the moment of death, and if looked at in this way the opening introduces an approach to time which involves reversal, as well as chronological development.

The image of snow falling is super-imposed, obscuring the boundary between inside the palace and outside. This abstract effect also blurs the boundary between the snow scene inside the paperweight and the world around Kane.

When Kane utters the word 'rosebud' and the paperweight tumbles to the floor, we become aware that this is a mysterious and significant object. The nurse's entry into the room is shown reflected in the paperweight. Kane's death is portrayed economically, with little information, and we have to assume that his last word was overheard. As the nurse draws the blanket over Kane's body we are aware of a figure who dies in isolation.

The mysteriousness of the opening sequence contrasts with the informative voice-over of the newsreel which follows immediately and provides a background of information to the enigmatic death seen in the opening sequence. It is also fast moving, inventive and engaging. The foreboding, nightmarish image of Xanadu is now replaced by images of extreme wealth showing that Xanadu is a luxurious estate. The enormous extent of Kane's wealth suggests that he saw himself as a mythical figure for the twentieth century. The voice-over compares him to Noah as we are told that he collected two of each species for his private zoo.

The newsreel, *News on the March*, shows the significance of Kane as a powerful international figure.

■ We learn how he acquired his fortune, and how his business empire developed and involved media interests. The problems posed to this empire are put in the context of real historical events, with reference, for instance, to the economic Depression in America during the 1930s.

■ We find out about his failed attempt to become involved in politics. When Kane himself appears in the newsreel, addressing reporters about his beliefs, we see his significance on the world stage. His ideas are made the subject of debate since he is accused of being a Communist by his financial guardian, Walter P. Thatcher, and a Fascist by a speaker at a rally of workers. Kane identifies himself as an 'American'.

■ His international significance is also demonstrated by a photograph which represents him in conversation with Hitler. Here is a sign that the film will present a critical portrait of the way Kane uses his power.

He is shown in 1935 speaking to a reporter about the Second World War in a way that emphasises Kane's age. His remarks to the interviewer are jokey and slightly patronising. Kane claims to have spoken with leaders from European countries, personally preventing the threat of war through his diplomacy.

Given that the film was released in 1941, prior to America's intervention in the war, viewers would be very aware of the hollowness of his claims to have resolved conflict in Europe.

■ The newsreel dramatically provides information about Kane's private life, showing how his first marriage collapsed – after the affair with Susan Alexander which ruined his political career – and how this was reported by the press. The voice-over also tells us that Kane's first wife Emily and his son were killed in a car crash two years after the collapse of the marriage, a tragic event which the narrative does not return to.

The *News on the March* sequence means that the film has made the daring move of suspending the introduction of a conventional narrative structure. When, in the following sequence, Rawlson urges his main reporter, Thompson, to investigate what Kane meant by his last word 'rosebud', a story-line is set up.

Like a detective film, the narrative now proceeds with an investigation. However, due to the nature of this investigation, in which the reporter gains more and more information about Kane's life, we cannot just compare the film with plot structures from the crime genre. In order to

lack of knowledge about Kane

Rawlson reacts dynamically to the screening of the newsreel, urging his reporters to look at Kane's life in greater depth. The darkness of the viewing room is both realistic and symbolic of the lack of knowledge about Kane possessed by the *News on the March* production team (see Style: Lighting)

gain a deeper understanding of how the narrative is structured we must first consider the pattern of cause and effect.

CAUSE AND EFFECT

Narratives involve a pattern of cause and effect and different approaches to the structure of this may radically alter our experience of a film. For example, the result of a particular cause may be delayed until later in the narrative, or not understood until towards the end of a film. Some films provide an ambiguous account of what causes events in the story to take place.

David Bordwell and Kristin Thompson (see Bibliography) emphasise how classical Hollywood cinema is based on providing the audience with a very clear understanding of cause and effect within the narrative (David Bordwell, Kristin Thompson, *Film Art: An Introduction*, Third Edition, pp. 70–1).

In *Citizen Kane*, despite the opening with Kane's death followed by the newsreel, a clear sense of cause and effect is established. The death of Kane leads to the newsreel which presents a report on his life and death. Then follows the problem of finding out what Kane's life meant in a deeper sense, prompted by the enigmatic 'rosebud' utterance. The newspaper editor's perception of this, as the starting point for an inquiry, leads to Thompson's interviews with the key figures who knew Kane.

Our understanding of cause and effect in the narrative is delayed, because we only learn how the newsreel and Kane's death fit into the film when the reaction of Rawlson and the other reporters is shown. The delay in revealing cause and effect allows the film to achieve the surprise created by the transition, through editing, from the shot of Kane's window to the loud arrival of the newsreel on screen.

David Bordwell also shows that classical Hollywood narrative is based on 'character-centred causality'. This means that, within Hollywood films, character aims are clearly shown as causes. This approach is used in *Citizen Kane*, where we can see the importance of Rawlson's motivation to discover the underlying story of Kane's life.

flashback structure

A structure is provided for the story even though Rawlson and his reporter, Thompson, are not developed as characters. The narrative's development, which follows the decision to investigate the meaning of 'rosebud', is unusually complex because of a return to the past organised through flashbacks.

Nevertheless the narrative still progresses coherently with Thompson piecing together the story of Kane's life, which in itself displays a sequence of cause and effect. The film alternates between Thompson's progress in collecting information from various memories of Kane and the story of Kane's life, which emerges from these memories. In these two parallel lines of narrative development Kane's story is dominant, while Thomson remains an anonymous figure. Like the viewer he absorbs the story which unfolds.

Through the flashback structure we witness Kane's desire to succeed as a newspaper owner and as a political candidate; these and his desire to see Susan triumph as an opera singer are at the forefront of the story. They are clearly established aims and through them we understand how they cause various events to happen, including the rise of *The Inquirer*; the clash with the political opponent Gettys; and the desperate attempts to promote Susan as a star.

In relation to the organisation of cause and effect, an important question is whether an explanation is offered for the various personality traits which Kane displays. A critical scene for this issue is that in which Kane is taken away from his childhood home by Walter P. Thatcher. The childhood scene establishes a conflict between Kane and his father and it is this, and his mother's reaction to it, which is presented as the cause of his departure. Kane's father threatens to thrash him, and his mother replies: 'That's why he's going to be brought up where you can't get at him'.

Looked at from a contemporary perspective where parent/child relationships have been scrutinised in greater depth, this scene appears to provide a disturbing cause for Kane's problems later in life. The film provides a minimal account of family as the source of Kane's adult problems. However, the revelation at the end that 'rosebud' refers to the sledge gives the childhood scene increased significance.

themes

As the story of Kane's life proceeds through the flashbacks our attention is focused on the force of Kane's personality as a cause of both his successes and his failures. The childhood scene also establishes the conflict between Kane and Thatcher, thus setting up the rebelliousness of *The Inquirer*. Kane's conflict with Thatcher is drawn out later in the flashback, based on Thatcher's memoir, where Kane's life is discussed in the wake of huge economic losses brought on by the Depression. Kane is asked by Thatcher what he would like to have been and says, 'Everything you hate'.

Kane's marriage to Emily Monroe Norton, and later to Susan Alexander, demonstrate that this film – like many other Hollywood films – puts the romantic aims of the main character at the centre of the story. Alongside the quest for success in the public sphere, Kane's relationships with both of these women are established as important in understanding his life. Yet Kane is never clearly established as a romantic hero, and the troubles and tragedies of the relationships are presented partly as the effect of his difficult personality.

This failure of the main protagonist presents a more complicated approach to classical narrative, since many Hollywood films aim to please their audiences with happy endings. Kane shares qualities with the typical hero, but is also a tragic figure. As a result, the film has a more complicated organisation of cause and effect. We cannot immediately be sure why Kane fails, but Leland is a decisive commentator on Kane's weaknesses pointing out that he failed to love anyone apart from himself.

One reason why Kane retains some sympathy is because the causes of his actions point to the need for a more psychological understanding of his character, rather than just a sense of good or evil. At the same time there is also the suggestion that he is a scoundrel who has no settled character but performs various roles. This again contrasts with the Hollywood emphasis on characters with sharply defined goals. Since this action is shown from the perspective of characters remembering the past, there is a greater sense of distance from Kane, and to an extent Kane's character remains mysterious (see Chronology and temporal order).

Although Kane's personality is established clearly during the first flashback the narrative is set up as an investigation into his character. We are given sufficient information to understand why he acts as he does, but a sense of enigma is maintained as the reporter presses on in the hope of finding out whether 'rosebud' represents an underlying truth about Kane's life.

The information which is withheld promises to be the secret to Kane's life. As well as presenting Kane as a dynamic figure who causes events to happen, the film presents an exploration of his personality. The narrative is carefully structured so that we are given moments of surprise despite the information provided at the beginning by the newsreel.

characterisation

We have seen how character motivation provides the basis of the narrative through Rawlson's quest to find the meaning of Kane's life and various ambitions (see Cause and effect). We will now look in more detail at:

■ How Kane's character changes.

■ How the film provides a balance between clearly defined character traits and a more open-ended ambiguous presentation of Kane's personality.

■ How some of the other characters are presented.

Although the film has a more political subject than many other Hollywood films, Kane's involvement in politics is ultimately related to personal qualities. The characterisation becomes more complex because vital information about Kane's life is withheld. We are left to imagine Kane as the radical newspaper owner attacking injustice, since this period is explored so economically by the film.

The withholding of information is most apparent in the question of what 'rosebud' meant for Kane. While the film successfully gives the viewer freedom to imagine Kane's character, the absence of information also shows a coldness. The aim of producing a story with epic scope is given precedence over vital information about characters. For instance the death of Kane's first wife and child is referred to in the newsreel,

signs of ruthless insensitivity

but the narrative does not have time to examine how this tragedy affected Kane.

Nevertheless, in some respects Kane has very consistent traits. The film depicts the public and private sides of Kane's power, through the exploration of his ambition and relationships. Kane's character emerges more fully through his interaction with others. He only changes due to ebbing fortunes as power is acquired and lost. This transformation is accompanied by a loss of integrity which is explored through the decline of Kane's friendship with Leland. His power becomes disturbing in the relationship with Susan as he forces her to continue her singing career to the point where she attempts suicide.

This is a brutal development from his early dominance in the offices of *The Inquirer*, although even here there are signs of ruthless insensitivity as the old editor is swept aside. The comic quality of the scenes depicting Kane's take-over of *The Inquirer* make the emphasis on his tyrannical qualities less explicit.

Xanadu represents the ultimate expression of Kane's drive towards total control and power, but it is also a retreat from the public world. He still has some of the qualities of a victim at this point, but the sense of pathos is not related to events outside his relationship with Susan.

The dialogue is a rich source of characterisation and ambiguous wordplay. Character conflict is expressed powerfully through particular speeches. The language used in the screenplay reveals psychological traits and is geared to the pace, action and drama of the narrative. At various points, the dialogue demonstrates different aspects of Kane's character: idealist; rebel; bully; charismatic enthusiast; victim; show-man, and the tragic protagonist.

In his first appearance as a young man, when Kane tells Walter P. Thatcher: 'The trouble is Mr Thatcher, you don't realise you're talking to two people', Kane evokes the idea that he is not a completely unified personality.

This line also introduces Kane's rhetorical style as he demonstrates to Thatcher a sympathy for the view that: 'Charles Foster Kane is a scoundrel', while asserting his rights as, 'the publisher of *The Inquirer*'.

characterisation narrative & form

At certain points events are referred to which do not take place in the story. Kane's role in attempting to provoke the Spanish-American war in Cuba is stated in the first scene at *The Inquirer*. Here his reply to the correspondent in Cuba is: 'Dear Wheeler – you provide the prose poems – I'll provide the war'. This illustrates Kane's unscrupulous use of power right from the beginning; and, since these lines duplicate a famous statement by Hearst, demonstrates how the screenplay specifically targeted him.

Later in the film Kane tells Thatcher: 'If I hadn't been rich I might have been a truly great man'. This line relates to the sense of Kane's unrealised potential, and the possibility that Kane is different from the public role he was forced to take.

The screenplay builds up a sense of ambiguity around Kane's character. However he is sufficiently consistent to be enigmatic rather than puzzling. The audience is encouraged to identify Kane as a character who changes, but is principally defined through his pursuit of power. In the sequence which shows his marriage with Emily Monroe Norton we see how he becomes dogmatic and argumentative. When Emily confronts Kane over his affair, his speech reflects a refusal to accept that Gettys has undermined him, stating: 'There's only one person in the world to decide what I'm going to do – and that's me'.

The individuality of each character who remembers Kane is revealed swiftly by the dialogue. Leland as an old man talks in a way that mixes intelligence with a degree of cynicism about Kane. We don't know the extent of his bitterness about what happened, instead we accept him as a thoughtful character who has survived Kane and the disappointments of the election defeat. Susan moves from silence to talkative confessional. Bernstein makes wry remarks on his position as chairman of the board, and tells an odd story about his memories of a girl in a white dress seen on the ferry.

The screenplay establishes that these characters have distinctive and subjective memories of Kane, but their roles are restricted so that the story of Kane's life takes centre stage and gathers a sense of continuity.

The other characters, like Kane, have clearly defined traits. To an extent the definition of these characters is related to their social and economic context. Thatcher, the banker is coldly formal and traditional in his outlook, and represents the impersonal authority of the capitalist establishment. Bernstein represents the shrewdness of the successful manager who loyally supports Kane, and nostalgically remembers the dynamism of the early days of *The Inquirer*. He is a comic and philosophical observer of life, but also displays wistful melancholy. Leland and Susan are more complex characters because they are more emotionally involved with Kane. They both change significantly during the story.

Leland, like Kane has a connection with inherited wealth, but in contrast he comes from a family where the fortune has disappeared. The political differences between Kane and Leland consist mainly of Leland's greater awareness of changes in society, away from a world where the powerful see their role as pre-ordained.

Leland's hostility to Kane, after the election, is made stronger by his feeling that Kane has shown aristocratic contempt for the voters with his irresponsibility in the Susan Alexander scandal. For instance, in the exchange between Leland and Kane after the election defeat, Leland criticises Kane's selfishness: 'The truth is, Charlie, you just don't care about anything except you. You just want to convince people that you love them so much that they should love you back. Only you want love on your own terms'.

Kane does not fully reply to this until later in the scene after Leland has requested to go to Chicago. The scene ends with Kane saying: 'A toast, Jedediah – to love on my own terms. These are the only terms anybody knows – his own'.

These words demonstrate Kane's egocentric view of the world and the decline of his friendship with Leland. We are left in doubt as to how much Kane ever managed to feel love.

The more extended conflict between Kane and Susan is shown mainly as a result of his bullying and obsessiveness. However, the conflict can also be understood in relation to class differences – Susan challenges Kane's use of his wealth to win her affection. But Kane's involvement with Susan shows a desire to return to the time of his youth, before the huge acquisition of status and wealth.

Susan is represented as being a more ordinary person than Emily (his first wife), unconnected to the establishment and the famous. Yet the relationship is shaped by Kane's increasingly crazy displays of wealth. Susan ultimately shows independence, walking away from the marriage, but displays a sense of inner conflict in the interview with Thompson. Having expressed her sense of independence in leaving Kane, she still shows grief over his demise.

Throughout the film all the actors increase the originality of the characterisation with lively, confident performances. Narrative development, conveyed through the screenplay, is emphasised by the actors using credible gestures and expression.

Kane's personality and relationship with other characters is also conveyed through the physical side of the acting, and during the political speeches we are made aware that Kane himself is a kind of actor. Welles draws on a range of facial expressions and other physical movements to represent Kane's transformation. In the shot which shows Kane after Susan's departure, Welles graphically depicts the sense of loss before his emotions are released with an attack on the objects in their bedroom.

chronology and temporal order

In a highly original way the flashbacks complicate the narrative so that a simple linear progression in time from one period to another is interrupted. From the narrative as a whole the viewer can reconstruct Kane's life chronologically, beginning in 1876 with his childhood, leading through his life events to his death, followed by Thompson's inquiry.

So what is the effect of having these events presented out of sequence? The main consequence of this approach is to make us aware that the story comes to us through other characters. Where a conventional approach to the **bio-pic** provides a sense of the individual's life being described from one perspective, in this film we are made aware that different personalities contribute to the story. Nevertheless there is still a sense of a singular story being recounted.

Thompson's inquiry proceeds through the life in a way that is almost completely linear. However, the temporal order is affected by the fact that Kane's story results from the memories of different people. The Thatcher memoir advances the story to 1929 when Kane's ownership of newspapers was affected by the Depression. This is shown before Bernstein's memories of *The Inquirer*'s rise as a newspaper. We are made aware that Thatcher's memoir concentrates more directly on economic issues.

There is an overlap between Leland's memory of the events leading to his dismissal for his negative review and Susan's memory of the opera performances – in the latter Leland is briefly shown as a figure in the audience tearing up his notepaper. Finally, Susan's account of her departure from Xanadu is connected with the story presented by Raymond the butler. In the story based on Susan's memory we see her leave down a seemingly endless corridor, but in Raymond's account we see Susan emerge from this corridor.

When each flashback is introduced the film suggests that what we see corresponds with the memories of the acquaintance who is talking. The dialogue preceding each flashback, apart from the one based on Thatcher's memoir, involves a remembering of the past. However, during each flashback events and actions are shown which exceed what the character responsible for the memories could have seen.

This is not used to cultivate doubt about the authenticity of the character's claims about Kane. It allows the audience, following the conventions of **classical Hollywood**, to interpret the flashback as a presentation which corresponds, through artistic licence, with the information provided by the character.

It is possible to question the absolute authority of the characters' memories because the film provides reasons why particular memories may be influenced by each character's own personal feelings – for instance, Leland and Susan have reasons to be hostile to Kane. However, the film does not accentuate the subjectivity of each person's memories.

While most films using a flashback structure concentrate on the memory of one character, *Citizen Kane* introduces the likelihood of more ambiguity by using five characters' memories; but the possibility of different versions of Kane's life is held back. Thompson plays an important role because we are given the impression he is constructing a continuous story.

The convention of using linear development in narratives is frequently connected with the idea of achievement by a central protagonist. The transition from one period to another allows achievement to be gauged, or, in the case of tragedy, failure to be measured.

The re-ordering of the narrative in *Citizen Kane* to include the death at the beginning, and an economic profile of the life-story in the newsreel, provides the audience with foreknowledge, a convention developed by classical Greek tragedy. By using flashbacks from different perspectives which are related to one another, we have a narrative that convincingly builds on the introduction of foreknowledge and incorporates the central protagonist's rise and fall.

If the film had made Kane a more positive character who simply achieves success there would have been less need for accounts of his life from different perspectives. But since the audience must be prepared for Kane's downfall, one benefit of using flashbacks is that the audience gains a greater distance from Kane, and the structure allows room for a more detached, neutral view of him.

In this respect, a relationship is maintained with the newsreel which presents a report on Kane's life. The flashback structure creates the scope for a varied, flexible form of story-telling, and establishes the psychological complexity which is frequently associated with European art films.

equilibrium & disequilibrium

These concepts refer to the viewer's experience of the film. Equilibrium describes those periods in which the viewer experiences a sense of calm or stability in relation to the fictional world.

In classical Hollywood films this state frequently corresponds to our empathy with central characters when they successfully achieve their principal goals, such as romantic union, or defeat of a villain. There is a sense that the main character(s) deserve the happiness which accompanies the successful achievement of their goals. To achieve equilibrium the viewer must identify or empathise with the main character (who is successful), and must also fully comprehend the story (which has been completed so that issues are resolved and the main sources of tension have been eliminated).

The usual practice with classical Hollywood films is to create a state of stability at the beginning of the film which provides a sense of equilibrium. This state is then disrupted by dramatic events or unresolved situations which present specific challenges to the main character(s).

Throughout the narrative there may be periods which can be interpreted as presenting equilibrium, but a sense of uncertainty about whether or how issues will be resolved is usually maintained until the end. Equilibrium is usually re-established at the end of the film, but this may involve significant changes from the steady state signified at the beginning.

Many films provide variations on this general model. *Citizen Kane* swiftly introduces disequilibrium through Kane's death, which is presented in a disturbing manner. The newsreel suggests a stronger sense of equilibrium as the voice-over provides a factual explanation of Kane's life and places him in context. However, questions remain and a sense of disequilibrium is enhanced because Kane's life remains mysterious.

The story of Kane's life, revealed through flashbacks, does not have the suspense of many Hollywood films because we already know, through the

Kane and Bernstein communicate during a celebratory dinner at *The Inquirer*. Kane's position as a charismatic leader is illustrated as the all-male team turn towards him. This still is also an example of how deep focus is used to represent grandeur and power.

newsreel, about key events in his life. Also we are distanced from Kane, so right from the start it is difficult for the viewer to either fully empathise with this character or feel satisfaction about his decline. Nevertheless, the narrative is still emotionally involving.

Significant emphasis at certain points on equilibrium or disequilibrium can be isolated. For instance, although Kane's childhood is not idyllic there is a strong sense of loss, emphasised by the shot of the sledge being covered in snow just after the arrangements have been made for Kane's departure. The film relates here to other myths and stories where the desired state of equilibrium is located in a rural, innocent world. This ideal is presented in many films directed by John Ford. However, in *Citizen Kane* this ideal is only presented economically by the mother's reference to the father's violence against his son.

Kane's steady but rapid progress with *The Inquirer* appears to provide a response to the disequilibrium signified through his conflict with Thatcher. The status of this section of the story – as an optimistic period in which Kane is more sympathetic – is only qualified by understated signs that his use of power could become unscrupulous. For instance, Kane's behaviour in these scenes already displays some signs of corruption. Significantly this apparently more stable period of his life is presented as the memory of Bernstein, whose committed work contributes to the success of *The Inquirer*.

The affair with Susan presents a decisive point and can be understood as fatally disrupting Kane's progress as a public figure of significance.

The ending of the film is ambiguous, and there is a sense of tragedy which prevents the kind of equilibrium produced when a hero/heroine achieves their goals. It can be argued that the film refuses to provide a sense of victory or defeat, instead we are given the impression that Kane's life has been more fully explained. This is made more complex because of the shot of the sledge.

Initially we may experience Thompson's final acceptance that the meaning of 'rosebud' is elusive as a satisfactory state of equilibrium. However, the

Leland, Kane and Bernstein gaze through
the window of *The Inquirer*'s building. The
prominence of the circulation figures leads
on to Kane's quest to challenge *The Inquirer*'s
more successful rival called *The New York Chronicle*

equilibrium

shot of the sledge which follows provides the viewer with a separation from Thompson's enquiry. The viewer is left to decide what the image of the sledge signifies.

It can be argued that a more satisfactory state of equilibrium is reached here since at last 'rosebud' is identified. The image does not provide the explanation sought by Rawlson. 'Rosebud' has mixed associations and can be related to conflict in Kane's life, but most directly the sledge refers to Kane's happiness as a child playing in the snow, free from the trappings of power. To what extent this provides equilibrium is open to debate.

style

mise-en-scène *p44*   **montage** *p55*   **the soundtrack** *p58*

mise-en-scène

Mise-en-scène is defined in *An Introduction to Film Studies* as: 'A theatrical term usually translated as "staging" or "what has been put into a scene". In film mise-en-scène refers not only to sets, costumes and props but also how the scene is organised, lit and framed for the camera. Mise-en-scène is one way of producing meaning in films which can be straightforward and extremely complex depending on the intentions and skill of the director.' (Jill Nelmes, ed., 'Glossary of Key Terms' in *An Introduction to Film Studies*, p. 434)

DEEP FOCUS

Film theorists have discussed the merits of different aspects of the film's style. Bazin, for instance emphasised the effects achieved through mise-en-scène. Bazin praised the use of wide-angle lenses because they allow for a greater 'openness' in the images; introduced 'tension' into the image through the contrast between foreground and background; and allowed greater depth of field. He championed the use of **deep focus** because this allowed shots in which details of the foreground and the background were kept in focus simultaneously.

For Bazin, this approach to film-making was progressive since it gave the viewer freedom to look at different parts of the shot and provided greater freedom for interpretation. According to this approach instead of cutting up a scene into different shots – which is the typical approach to scene construction in **classical Hollywood** cinema – a different approach is favoured in which the unity of film space should be preserved as fully as possible.

Editing is very important throughout the film, but Bazin's argument is that specific shots involve a unique form of composition which contrasts aesthetically with the effects achieved through editing.

CITIZEN KANE

In *Citizen Kane* various means are used to preserve the space of individual shots where we might expect editing to intervene. Some scenes consist of only one shot, such as the one depicting Susan in bed following her suicide attempt. In other scenes considerable camera movement is used as an alternative to **cutting**. A good example here is the **tracking shot** over Kane's possessions to the fireplace in the penultimate scene. There are very few close-ups in *Citizen Kane*.

Deep focus is used to make single takes more detailed and it allows individual shots to set up more complex relationships between characters – in contrast to restricted use of depth which provides less scope for depicting physical distance. Physical distance becomes a very dynamic aspect of the film, contributing to our understanding of the characters and their relationships.

Citizen Kane uses aspects of the mise-en-scène and deep focus to make the story more 'realistic' than other films made at the time. The inclusion of ceilings (made possible by special low-angle shots), detailed interiors and complex visual backgrounds (made possible by deep focus) are some of the main ways in which the film strives to resemble 'real life'. This does not mean that the audience loses an awareness of the difference between fact and fiction. *Citizen Kane* is self-consciously an artistic version of reality.

In his account of working on the film Toland emphasised the quest for **'realism'.** However, the techniques used make the viewer more aware of how style is used to construct the film, and this style can equally be described as theatrical. Welles had substantial experience of directing plays in which a dynamic relationship between parts of the space becomes important. The attempt to make the fictional world more life-like is partly an experiment in style, but it is also intended to make the audience more absorbed in the fiction that is created.

SPACE AND FRAMING

Cutting is deliberately avoided in the childhood scene when Kane's mother discusses the arrangements for his departure from home with Thatcher. A tracking shot keeps these two characters and the husband in frame and in

mise-en-scène

mise-en-scène   style

conflict and ambiguity

focus as they move across the room talking. There is framing within the frame and use of deep focus as Kane is shown through a window playing in the background. His image is blurred slightly by the snow, but in relation to most other films at the time the juxtaposition within a single shot of two distinct areas of action, both involving movement, is spectacular.

Although our interpretation is relatively fixed by the narrative content, the composition within the single shot allows the viewer to contemplate the complexity of the relationships involved between the different characters. From the way the characters are positioned within the space, we are given the freedom to relate the difficult situation faced by Mrs Kane to Kane's freedom as a child.

The situation being represented involves conflict and ambiguity. Kane's father protests that he has a right to keep his son, but his words are over-ridden by those of his wife and Thatcher. Meanwhile, Kane can be heard in the background.

The dialogue, which at certain points involves overlapping, has a similar effect to the positioning of characters in the space and allows various elements to compete with one another for the viewer's attention. Tension is built up significantly within the single shot in which there is a degree of openness, so that sympathy could be felt for the father, or at least our judgement is partially suspended.

Nevertheless the mother's concern for her son contrasts with the father's desperate attempts at intervention.

The camera-work and framing make us aware of the difficulty of the situation and more sympathetic to the mother as, in this shot, she moves closer to the position of the camera, holding back her feelings of imminent loss.

The mother's authority within this scene is enhanced by the fact that she moves across to open the window, ensuring communication with her son, after the father has closed the window. It is only after editing has been introduced into the scene that the full conflict emerges between father and son, mother and father, and Kane and Thatcher. Editing is used to show the conflict outside in separate shots, while framing and the use of deep space create a stronger sense of unresolved tension in the house.

46   CITIZEN KANE

Deep focus and the character positioning is used to present changes of character. When Kane holds a celebration at *The Inquirer* he starts dancing with women he has hired to perform. As the scene progresses Leland and Bernstein are shown together in the foreground of a shot which emphasises their position as spectators. The use of a wide-angle lens, which holds them both in medium close-up, gives the impression that they are compressed into the image and this contributes to a feeling of uneasiness, depicting the separation of Kane from his closest allies.

The scene becomes more complicated in terms of visual composition, because when Leland starts talking to Bernstein, Kane is shown in the background – in the window reflection – dancing with the women. This image alternates with a reverse angle which actually shows Kane dancing with the women behind Leland and Bernstein.

The set-up echoes the scene from Kane's childhood because, as in that scene, the two characters in the foreground discuss Kane's future while he is in the background. (Leland tells Bernstein of his fears that Kane is forsaking his own ideas of how to run a newspaper to competition with the *New York Chronicle*. The celebration has been brought about by Kane's acquisition of journalists from the rival paper.) However, unlike the situation in childhood, where Kane is innocent and his business future organised for him, the scene at *The Inquirer* registers that Kane is more responsible for his own fate.

The loss of innocence is reflected in the loss of the extreme depth which we find in the childhood scene. Furthermore the editing of the shot showing Kane actually in the background, with the shot showing his reflection, produces a sense of his character being doubled by an image of him. There is also a change from the childhood scene because, where Kane was previously shown through an open window, now he is a reflection in a closed window.

Both the childhood scene and *The Inquirer* scene convey different stages in Kane's loss of freedom. The organisation of screen space contributes substantially to the cinematic expression of Kane's loss of integrity and the beginning of his tragic decline.

There are scenes throughout the film in which deep focus is used to give

mise-en-scène style

Enormous posters depicting Kane's political
campaign represent the increasing attempts
at self-promotion which accompany his bid
for political office

action and scenery dramatic significance. These include the single-shot scene showing Susan after her suicide attempt and the scenes depicting the conversations between Susan and Kane at Xanadu.

Another factor introduced by the use of deep focus is the attention to detail which is not directly significant to the story but contributes atmosphere or 'realism'. For instance, the scenes in the offices of *The Inquirer* show some details of the environment as a work place.

SETTING, DÉCOR, COSTUME AND MAKE-UP

A wide range of settings are used in keeping with the development of a story of epic scope. Three contrasting sets are: the cold, corporate grandeur of the Thatcher building; the industrious, crowded rooms of *The Inquirer*; the gloomy, lavish interiors of Xanadu. These settings help to develop our understanding of the characters and the narrative.

Thatcher's building corresponds with the alienation that Kane must have felt being brought up by a financial guardian. *The Inquirer* is the setting for Kane's triumphant rise as he brings dynamism to a business lacking in ambition, but it is also quite claustrophobic. The Gothic rooms of Xanadu suggest the madness that Kane leads his second wife into, separate from any normal lifestyle.

Another setting which is used to develop our sense of a character is Susan's nightclub. It is both a refuge for Susan from the alienating spaces of Xanadu, and a melancholy environment. In the two scenes which show the club, the customers have already left, and Susan sits alone showing a sense of grief for Kane's death.

Aspects of the décor contribute to characterisation, and the film's artistic complexity. The 'K' emblem on the gates of Xanadu identifies the location, but also could be interpreted as suggesting that Kane has in a way lost the normality of his full name and like a kind of figurehead has adopted a straightforward emblem to identify his property.

The posters in *The Inquirer* office represent the realistic details of Kane's political campaign. We see the posters when the campaign has failed so that the office environment increases our awareness of Kane's failure, and we are made more aware of how the newspaper was used to promote his political ambitions.

The sets draws specifically on real-life examples with the closest parallel being the relationship of Xanadu to Hearst's palace San Simeon. However, we can also see the influence of expressionism. In general, expressionist films were known for their use of specific lighting techniques in conjunction with a style of acting and use of setting to create a stronger sense of atmosphere (see Cultural contexts).

Following the style developed by film-makers in this tradition, objects and background details demonstrate Kane's excessive materialism which reaches the point of madness. There is ambiguity in the Xanadu section, because the viewer is not explicitly guided towards an interpretation of Kane as a figure who is lifelike in the extremity of his actions, or towards an understanding of him as a mythical, fantasy figure.

Both responses are possible and co-exist. The multiple mirrors in Xanadu demonstrate Kane's extravagant materialism, but they also convey a sense of his psychological disintegration. Here, since mirrors are a popular element of décor in films, *Citizen Kane* provides a variation on a standard device for increasing the psychological complexity of a leading character.

Occasionally objects are given momentary prominence within the staging of events. When Leland hears that Kane has lost the election, the film lingers briefly on the doors to a saloon where Leland disappears to drown his sorrows. This is followed by a brief image of the printer's type-set prepared to celebrate Kane's victory at the polls before the camera moves up to show Bernstein accepting, with resignation, that a different front page is necessary.

While editing is used here to develop the narrative – the contrast between the reactions of Leland and Bernstein – attention is also given to slightly unusual, independent details of the scenery. Costume and make-up play a role in representing character, identity and transformation.

In an interview with Peter Bogdanovich, Welles said that he would sometimes arrive on the set at 2.30 a.m. in order to be made up for the day's shooting. He was even made up to seem younger for the early scenes at *The Inquirer*. Other characters needed less make-up or none at all. In contrast to Welles, Everett Sloane, playing Bernstein, just had his hair cut back for the scenes of old age. This works because Bernstein is portrayed as a consistent character who remains loyal to Kane.

Costume is used to signify the political and social context of the narrative. Thatcher's top hat and formal attire establish his identity as a city businessman whose appearance contrasts with the simple clothes of Kane's parents. Kane himself is a smart, formal dresser. At the point where he announces his engagement, the white suit contributes to the appearance of a change taking place in his life following his holiday romance.

LIGHTING

The style of lighting is guided by a mixture of influences, including expressionism, Hollywood conventions, and the desire to forge a more realistic approach. It is used throughout in relation to narrative development and characterisation.

For some of the film, lighting is used in a way that conformed with standard Hollywood practice in the classical era. This involves ensuring that characters are fully illuminated to maintain accessibility for the audience. In a number of scenes lighting is used unobtrusively to present the narrative as clearly as possible. However, different lighting techniques were necessary to incorporate the use of ceilings.

During many scenes, shadow is used expressively and there are many examples of lighting being used to establish a contrast between shadow and full illumination of characters in a particular scene.

In *Citizen Kane*, as in film noir, low-key lighting is used to create shadows and atmospheric effects. The use of shadow contributes to a sense of gloom. Although the plot involves an investigation, the style of lighting is related to the tragic, mysterious qualities of Kane's life rather than the crime-based thriller narrative which we find in film noir.

In relation to production costs a general similarity exists between noir and *Citizen Kane* because both sought a less expensive mode of film-making through their distinctive approach to lighting. In *Citizen Kane* the grandeur and expanse of Xanadu was achieved on a relatively restricted budget,

Xanadu is represented here as a lavish palace, but
the empty spaces and Susan's preoccupation with the
fragments of a jigsaw evoke a sense of alienation.
The shadows are both 'realistic' and
express a sense of foreboding.

partly because the use of darkness through shadow makes the viewer imagine the space, based on what can be seen.

The opening sequence establishes a preoccupation with darkness as, prior to Kane's death, the night-time sequence conveys foreboding and a sense of mystery. When the newsreel reporters are shown after the screening of the newsreel, their faces are hidden in the darkness of the viewing room. By staging a conversation in this environment, the film defies the usual studio practice of providing full illumination for the main action.

The decision to show the scene in this way can be understood as a commitment to 'realism', but also the darkness can be interpreted as expressing the reporters' lack of knowledge. At the end, the group who gather around Thompson are also cast in shadow. Again this might signify a lack of knowledge, since the meaning of 'rosebud' remains undisclosed and Thompson's quest has come to an end.

Alternatively, the shadow could be regarded as a natural consequence of the huge, cavernous room which the group walk through. As elsewhere, the film creates different possibilities in terms of audience interpretation. The lighting clearly breaks with the high-key style associated with most Hollywood genres.

It can be argued that in a number of scenes, lighting is used to convey a sense that Kane is a tragic figure brought down by fatal weaknesses in his character. When Kane signs his Declaration of Principles he is cast in darkness, as if anticipating his failure in the future to maintain this commitment.

In contrast, Leland in the background is clearly lit. In the scene where Kane is confronted by Gettys and Susan with their knowledge of his affair, Kane is shown in darkness as he decides not to leave with his wife. He then steps into a position where his face is illuminated as the other characters react to his decision.

In the scene where Kane decides to finish the negative review of his wife's performance, a shadow is cast over the edges of his face. This suggests the rage he feels and also conveys the strangeness of his actions, completing the review in negative terms. The shadow does not distract from the film's interest in 'realism' since the scene occurs at night, but the shadow also original visual images

heightens the sense of drama. A feeling of doom is conveyed since Kane's decision to fire his friend occurs while he is typing the review. It is a critical moment in Kane's loss of integrity.

Shadow is also used in the scene where Kane confronts Susan about continuing with her singing after the first performance. The shadow which falls over Susan's face conveys how menacing Kane is at this point and dramatises her fear of what he might do. It suggests a disturbing level of violence hidden behind his public persona. The shadow marks a transition in Kane's character, making him seem more unpredictable. When Kane strikes Susan after she has confronted him in the tent, her face moves into shadow as she turns away from his slap.

Light (the image of natural light) is used as a powerful element during two early scenes. When we first see the sign of El Rancho, Susan's nightclub, lightning strikes as the neon writing and the image of Susan Alexander is illuminated. When Thompson inspects the manuscript at Thatcher's library, light floods down from a window at the top of the room acting as part of the spectacular setting.

These original visual images depend on the staging of lighting effects within the story. In each case our attention is drawn to the distinctiveness of the setting, but also the lighting contributes to the representation of character. Thatcher is presented as an integral part of the American élite and his building reflects this. The lighting of the El Rancho sign follows immediately after Rawlson's statement: 'Rosebud dead or alive! It will probably turn out to be a very simple thing'.

The juxtaposition of this statement with the sign can be interpreted as suggesting that Susan Alexander may be the key to the search which is initiated. By the end of the narrative we know that this is not the case, but in the moment where the sign is illuminated the spectacular association of the woman with mystery is a reminder that *Citizen Kane* shares some qualities with film noir. Another understanding of this lighting effect is that it heightens our curiosity about the relationship between Kane and Susan.

montage

As with other Hollywood films the editing in *Citizen Kane* is guided by the requirement of providing continuity. This was made more challenging by the dramatic shifts in time, resulting from the long period covered by the story and the flashback structure. The film makes inventive use of dissolves to increase the sense of continuity, to mark the unusual shifts in the time scheme, and to allow the story to unfold poetically.

Even more striking is the influence of 'montage'. This style of editing drew on the inspiration of Soviet film-makers such as Eisenstein (see Cultural contexts). Montage editing usually involves the unexpected combinations of short-length shots to create meaning for the spectator.

In *Citizen Kane* it is used to confront the viewer with surprise juxtapositions of different time periods, different spaces, and aspects of the mise-en-scène. However, the film strives to maintain continuity while using montage and its influence is most clearly seen in those sequences which present narrative developments elliptically.

The newsreel sequence provides a form of montage using short-length shots on general themes in Kane's life. The voice-over of the newsreel anchors the meaning provided by the range of images, while a rapid succession of shots shows, for instance, the different sources of Kane's power as an industrialist.

At certain points the rapid combination of diverse images encourages comparison, and this appears to be achieved without editing when we see – in quick succession – numerous newspaper headlines telling the story of Kane's death. This segment is close in style to other Hollywood adaptations of the montage technique. There is no attempt to achieve the political form of communication found in some Soviet films, but the rapid succession of different headlines conveys the general message that the death is international news.

More importantly, in relation to the original montage idea of allowing the viewer to compare images, the variety of photographs depicting different portraits of Kane is an innovative introduction to this multi-faceted character. The use of still images introduces a juxtaposition purely at the formal level, with the clips used in the newsreel and the movement involved in the rest of the film. These montage effects remain decorative because our attention is focused on the content of the story as a rapid amount of information is provided.

A number of other sections in the film are either influenced by montage or are innovative in relation to Hollywood's adoption of montage. We will look at four examples:

1. The section where Thatcher reacts to the development of *The Inquirer* is portrayed through a quick succession of shots. The sequence compresses a development which occurs over a period of time which is not exactly specified. Thatcher's presence in each shot, and the accompanying soundtrack, become dominant and unify the alternation between different locations. This allows the sequence to emphasise the comic nature of Thatcher's reaction.

   Through the rapid cutting from one shot to the next we get a sense of Thatcher's rising consternation at *The Inquirer's* attack on a land-owning trust. The sequence with its juxtaposition of different headlines also expresses in an economic way the development of *The Inquirer* as a campaigning paper.

   The sequence is made more unusual when Thatcher looks directly at the camera as if expressing his dismay to the audience. This form of direct address is found in some Hollywood films, such as musicals where a singer might look directly at the camera. However, this kind of effect is not generally included in mainstream cinema because it may disrupt the viewer's role as onlooker of the fictional world.

2. The sequence depicting the gradual deterioration of Kane's marriage with Emily Norton condenses nine years into a few minutes by rapidly progressing through six extracts of typical conversations which the couple have at the breakfast table. Each conversation involves a shot/reverse shot pattern, and to signify the passing of time costume, make-up and scenery change in each extract.

   As well as suggesting that the couple spend very little time together, the sequence charts the increasing sense of indifference. Each statement from Kane encapsulates a new attitude towards his wife which can be understood as a decline of affection. Equally Emily's statements reflect her increasing annoyance at some of Kane's actions with *The Inquirer*.

In the style of montage we are not given complete conversations but short extracts which signify a more extended process. While at the beginning the couple are shown close to each other, by the end they are separated by a long table.

The sequence is framed by Leland's comments. The location of the breakfast table relates to his observation that this was a marriage like any other marriage, because the breakfast table signifies a domestic side to Kane's existence. Leland's comments, which suggest that along with domestic familiarity boredom and hostility developed, could be considered cynical and the viewer is left to decide whether they are accurate. However, the fragmented nature of the section, with its reliance on the idea that these were typical moments in the marriage, means that it illustrates Leland's judgement while providing further details in the Kane story.

Of course, Leland was not present at the breakfast table, so the sequence already has the status of an imaginative reconstruction. Leland's image overlaps with the first and last image of the sequence, reinforcing the idea that this is his version of the events. Since we are not encouraged to see Leland as a fabricator or as fallible, the progress of the sequence presents Leland's account without questioning its accuracy.

3. The use of montage presents a disturbing sequence showing Susan's final performances at the opera. Here images of Susan, the audience, Kane as a spectator, the singing instructor, a glaring light and newspaper headlines are superimposed on the screen to represent the trauma experienced by Susan which leads to her suicide attempt.

4. Susan's recovery and defiance of Kane is powerfully evoked by being presented in stages over two flashbacks. When she is shown outside Xanadu the shot is introduced by a screaming parakeet (with a transparent eye), which amplifies the expression of the traumatic collision which has taken place.

This example of continuity is achieved in an unusual manner since the shot relates to her departure in the previous flashback. It also shows the creative use of surprising juxtaposition which forces the viewer towards a more active interpretation of Susan's breakup with Kane.

The idea of montage relates mainly to juxtaposition between shots but, as Eisenstein suggested, the principle can occur within a shot. The parakeet offers a surprising juxtaposition in relation to the previous shot and in relation to Susan walking away. Montage within a single shot offers a point of connection with contrasts achieved through deep focus.

the soundtrack

Throughout the film music is used in a way that is both respectful of Hollywood conventions and innovative. For instance, the music is used conventionally to create a stronger sense of narrative continuity where the editing follows a montage pattern.

As Claudia Gorbman points out, the music in the breakfast table sequence signifies both continuity in the marriage and the changes which occur in the relationship between Kane and Emily (Claudia Gorbman, *Unheard Melodies: Narrative Film Music*, p. 26). The continuity of the music over scenes that register five different time-sequences makes this section more effective as the exploration of a theme – the increasing emotional coldness between husband and wife.

As Gorbman and others have explained, it is normal for classical Hollywood film to use music as a way of enhancing continuity as well as providing a powerful form of expression. In an interview with the *New York Times*, Bernard Herrmann, the composer, discussed how the soundtrack contained two recurring motifs – one to signify Kane's power, the other with reference to 'rosebud'.

Kane's power is first expressed by music as we see Xanadu in the opening scene, and the rosebud motif is expressed when Kane utters the word 'rosebud' as he dies. Both motifs are repeated with variations at different points in the film to develop our understanding of Kane as a character.

Different forms of music are used not only to signify thematic developments, but also historical changes. For instance, the waltz – a popular musical form of the late nineteenth century – is used in the scene where Kane celebrates his acquisition of staff from *The Chronicle*.

The music is also used to convey different moods. When the soundtrack refers to Kane's power a sense of foreboding is evoked on frequent occasions. This is the case during the opening shots of Xanadu. By contrast the music which introduces Thatcher's memoir, with the sequence on the snow, is uplifting and lyrical. Here the music expresses Kane's freedom as a child. The music conveys the pleasure of a time when Kane was not caught up in the trappings of power.

The distinction between diegetic and non-diegetic music allows us to understand how the music is used for very different purposes within the film. Music is diegetic when what we hear is music produced within the film's fictional world. This is the case, for instance, with the scene that involves music from the band and dancers in the office of *The Inquirer*.

In sections of the film depicting the opera, the music is also diegetic but it moves to a more abstract level, and sounds relating to various performances are combined thus contributing to the general sense of a cacophony in individual performances.

Non-diegetic music cannot be traced to a source within the fictional world of a film; the music only relates to what is happening on screen in terms of meaning. In this instance, the soundtrack may be used to provide a musical evocation of feelings that are relevant to the characters and action; or to build up atmosphere, as in the case of the soundtrack for the opening sequence of *Citizen Kane*.

Non-diegetic music can have an authority which other voices in the film do not have. For most of *Citizen Kane*, however, this authority is not used to undermine any of the individual narrators who contribute to the story of Kane's life. In general, the non-diegetic music complements the meaning created by the various elements, and contributes to the coherence of this fictional world.

However, at the end of the film when the sledge is introduced the music heightens the sense of a revelation which eludes all the characters. Here, the music appears to challenge all the explanations offered about Kane and instead communicates directly to the viewer. This moment can be interpreted as overt authorial expression. Herrmann and Welles worked in close collaboration on the relationship of the music to the shooting of the film.

Sound, like music, is used as a source of continuity and for expressive effect. When Kane stands with Bernstein and Leland in front of a photograph showing the staff at *The Chronicle*, the next shot seems at first to represent a continuation of speech. A verbal link is used to bridge six years.

Commenting on another point where a verbal link is used in the film Alan Rowe states:

> Welles uses Thatcher's Merry Christmas as a bridge between Kane's boyhood greeting and adulthood. Such extravagant devices do not, however, disguise transitions in the way of continuity editing, but rather celebrate it.
>
> *Alan Rowe in Jill Nelmes (ed), An Introduction to Film Studies, p. 110*

In other words, at this point, the sound is used in an innovative, playful way which draws attention to the film's form. This happens in addition to the more functional purpose of developing the story. At most points our attention as viewers is focused on particular characters speaking without interference of background noise.

However, when the reporters gather round after the newsreel has been shown they all speak at once. Since the isolation of individual speech is used as a matter of convention throughout a dramatic film story, this overlapping dialogue is further evidence of a striving for greater realism. However, at this particular point in the narrative of *Citizen Kane,* the mass of voices is chiefly used to convey a sense of confusion.

A different type of soundtrack mixing occurs when thunder is followed by jazz as the camera moves from outside Susan's nightclub to inside with a crack of lightning playfully included as the camera appears to go through the skylight. Here the effect is one of extravagant style. Sound is used to complement the use of deep focus. When Kane is shown playing in the background snow, we still hear his voice shouting 'the union forever'. At Xanadu his voice seems to boom in the depths of the room as he approaches Susan constructing her jigsaw.

The voice-over in the newsreel is an obvious example of sound anchoring the meaning of the images. However, to an extent, the newsreel is presented paradoxically. Like the various speeches about Kane's life, the newsreel does not have absolute authority. There is a sense in which the other means of narration, such as camera-work, editing, mise-en-scène and, as mentioned above, non-diegetic sound provide independent access to the meaning of the images.

A consistent idea guiding the use of sound in mainstream cinema is that it should anchor the meaning provided by the images. It corresponds with what is seen on the image track. Welles's background in radio, in conjunction with Herrmann's creativity as a composer, meant that *Citizen Kane* is unusually subtle and complex in the use of sound. Where other film-makers might allow the soundtrack to play a more restricted role, here it is used to develop the detail of the fictional world in a very original way.

At other points it is used to create an elaborate, playful style which contributes to the development of the narrative themes.

contexts

ideology *p62*   **production history** *p67*   **cultural contexts** *p75*
the audience *p82*   **critical responses** *p84*   **conclusion** *p87*

ideology

The concept of ideology has several meanings. Initially we will concentrate on ideology as a concept – meaning a set of ideas or a belief system which has significant influence within society. The concept can be used critically to challenge and question ideas or beliefs which may appear to be natural.

Citizen Kane provides a critical portrait of Kane's rise to power and arguably undermines the belief that a person should have this power without being democratically accountable. In doing this, the film also raises questions about the role of big business. Although Kane rebels against the character Thatcher, he does not challenge the capitalist beliefs which Thatcher represents and the hostility is mainly represented as being personal.

As the newsreel reveals, Kane becomes a mighty capitalist and a dominant figure within American society; and in the film we see how Kane uses his power selfishly and in an unprincipled way. This is illustrated by his use of the newspaper to promote Susan's career and his conflict with Leland, who seems to have a greater commitment to progressive politics.

The film does not show Kane changing political views as Hearst did with his move from radical beliefs to reactionary views. Nevertheless Kane's political views are challenged. At the rally he speaks for the 'underprivileged' but appears to concentrate more on opposing Gettys' policies rather than holding forth on his own. Lack of firm convictions is one of Leland's strongest accusations against Kane.

The conflict between these two characters becomes irresolvable when the election is lost due to the Susan Alexander scandal. Leland's anger, in the scene where he drunkenly confronts Kane, progresses to accusations of political naïvety. The latter, Leland suggests, is effectively out of touch with the people he was standing for. Ego has led Kane to be too concerned with his own interests. Leland suggests that soon there will be a new force in American politics based on the organisation of the working classes themselves, and they will no longer have to rely on the actions of a powerful liberal.

Leland's argument with Kane provides a challenge also to the latter's belief in his rights as an individual. When Kane proposes a toast 'to the idea of love on your own terms', adding that these are 'the only terms that anyone knows' he resolutely maintains his belief in his right as an individual to decide his own fate (see Narrative and form: Characterisation).

The film allows the viewer to decide on this position, but the stubbornness of Kane's behaviour relates to his decision not to stand down from the election for the sake of his family. Kane's stubbornness is also shown in his subsequent abuse of power in running the newspaper to promote Susan Alexander's career as a singer.

When Leland returns the Declaration of Principles after being sacked, it is a sign that the ideal of honest reporting for the people has become exposed. Kane's behaviour can now be interpreted as either very selfish and/or tyrannical.

By making the central character flawed, *Citizen Kane* provides a contrast with so many Hollywood films in which the power of the individual is justified through an heroic protagonist. Orson Welles is known to have held left-wing, liberal views and to have sympathised with Roosevelt's New Deal government, with its social democratic political philosophy and emphasis on a welfare programme for ordinary people. This accords with the film's challenge to the extreme power of figures, such as Hearst, and their belief in *laissez faire* freedom for the individual.

Welles's beliefs also explain why Kane's opposition to Thatcher and, at the beginning of his career, the politically progressive use of *The Inquirer's* challenge to corrupt landlords, is presented with some sympathy. When Kane stands for political office he makes it clear that he is attacking an authoritarian 'boss', Jim Gettys. (The term 'boss' was used to refer to powerful individuals who, in nineteenth-century American politics, began to play a dominant role by their control over different interest groups, including businesses and the unions.) Thus Kane's challenge to Gettys partly represents the appeal for an alternative to corruption in politics.

There are many reasons why an outright attack on a tycoon would have been tempered. Herman Mankiewicz, for instance, did not share Orson Welles's passion for progressive causes. This explains why the screenplay incorporates the satire on a personal level, which angered Hearst. If Kane had been modelled, more abstractly, on the idea of a media mogul, the wealthy individuals behind Hollywood – and R.K.O. in particular – might have vetoed the project.

Welles had no interest in producing a film to challenge the power of Nelson Rockefeller, who had financial control over R.K.O. Likewise, anticipation of reprisals by Hearst may have prevented an even more direct personal attack on his use of the press for sensational reporting.

A problem which we face in considering the film in relation to ideology, is that it is frequently difficult to explain a film purely as the expression of political views – or other kinds of belief – held at the time of production. Since Hollywood was a capitalist industry, committed to making profits, it was unlikely to produce that many films which challenged the prevailing ideas of the society. This explains why *Citizen Kane* concentrates on the abuse of power by an individual, rather than individualism in capitalist society or class conflict.

After 1941 the aims of the industry, and the Government, converged more dramatically as propaganda became vital to the Government's intervention in the Second World War. It can be argued that *Citizen Kane* relates to this trend of greater co-operation with the Government, since, at that time, Hearst was opposed to the Government and intervention in the Second World War.

As Laura Mulvey argues, the film provides an intimation of the threat posed by Fascism through the portrait of Kane's extreme power and, at another level, suggests the inadequacy of non-intervention through, for example, Kane's speech in the newsreel where he claims to have averted the war (Laura Mulvey, *Citizen Kane*, p. 39, p. 75). However, these political points are submerged within the film's emphasis on personalities and artistic experiment.

The concept of ideology has also been used to show how films, through their aim to reach wide audiences, place greater emphasis on entertainment, artistic expression and story-telling, rather than political analysis. In relation to this perspective, *Citizen Kane* is very open to debate. To an extent the film fails to challenge dominant ideas because of its commitment to art and entertainment. At another level it can be argued that the innovative style of the film provides an alternative to the dominant ways in which films usually represented society.

Taking this into account, it can be argued that the innovative nature of the film made viewers more aware of how film language can be used in diverse ways to create meanings. Although this did not present a direct challenge to dominant ideas in society, it did inspire many film-makers and critics to look for alternatives to the dominant style of Hollywood cinema.

In particular, the use of **flashbacks** raised the possibility of exploring, with different perspectives and conflicting views, the historical context of contemporary political issues in a more complex fashion.

GENDER IN CITIZEN KANE

By concentrating so overwhelmingly on a man's story the film maintains a bias towards a male subject and we need to look specifically at how it represents gender. It can be argued that the flawed character of the central protagonist undermines the patriarchal ideology of the strong male hero. Another difference, from many other commercial films, is that there is little presentation of female characters as objects for a male voyeuristic gaze.

Laura Mulvey argues that in the opera sequence, when Susan is on stage as a performer, the viewer is made aware of Kane's idealised view of his wife and this undermines the possibility that she is simply an object for the gaze of the male spectator.

To understand how the film presents gender, we must consider in greater detail how the female characters are constructed. Emily Monroe Norton and Susan Alexander are both portrayed in a way that seeks to be 'realistic'.

Emily is represented as respectable and conservative, and the breakdown of the marriage between Kane and Emily is portrayed economically. We can see that Kane is dogmatic and obsessed with his work, while Emily is perhaps too much a part of the Establishment to appreciate his radical views. However, we know that Kane is ambitious and when the marriage collapses, due to his infidelity, his lack of responsibility is shown to be the crucial cause of the split. He fails to leave Susan's flat with Emily, despite the fact that Gettys and both women think that he should do this.

To an extent Emily is represented as a strong character, confronting her husband over his infidelity, but her strength seems to come from her powerful and wealthy background. More importantly the film represents her emotional response minimally, turning the absence of emotion in her reactions into a brief portrayal of disenchanted composure.

Susan's decision to walk away from Kane is a demonstration of female independence. She is able to turn away from the wealth which her marriage to Kane involves. The break-up of this relationship stems from Kane's actions. From the start he turns Susan's desire to be a singer into a relentless, ambitious quest, without sensitivity to her feelings.

In the shot which shows Susan after her suicide attempt, lying in bed, Kane is shown entering the room in the background. Arguably the **deep focus** reinforces the connection between both figures and the glass in the foreground, drawing attention to Kane's responsibility for the suicide attempt.

After Susan's recovery she is still troubled by Kane's heartless approach and complains about the conditions at Xanadu. The montage of jigsaws suggests how Susan keeps boredom at bay, and also evokes the ongoing theme of fragmentation (principally in their relationship).

The representation of Susan concentrates on her unhappiness. When she leaves Kane, we see a female doll figure on the left of the image which suggests that Kane has ceased to treat her as a person. Her character is not a stereotype, but with further development she could have represented an even stronger challenge to the problems of power and greed associated with Kane.

The other woman of significance in this story, is Kane's mother. Agnes Moorhead plays this role in a way that conveys steely conviction in acting the best way for her son. There is a strong sense of withheld remorse as she tells Thatcher that: 'I've got his trunk all packed – (she chokes a little) I've had it packed for a couple of weeks – '.

The female characters, therefore, have a certain amount of power within the story, and the characterisation seeks to convey 'realistic' and ambiguous psychological traits in opposition to exaggerated caricature. The same enigmatic openness, which occurs with the presentation of Kane, applies to all three portraits. Each involves a tension between what we know and what we do not know.

The covert narration informs us about the death of Emily and Kane's son through the newsreel without exploring Kane's feelings. This indicates the male protagonist's alienation, but also means that the film deals with the tragedy in a cold manner. Similarly Susan's suicide attempt is shown very economically.

The film's emphasis on the epic scope of Kane's life involves a restricted representation of overpowering emotional issues raised by his relationship with the female characters. The film concentrates on the bleakness of Kane's character and does not develop a stronger contrast between his domineering behaviour and the female characters.

We are left with the images of Emily as the conservative wife who Kane cheats on; Susan as the mistress, turned wife, who only rebels after being driven to the point of self-destruction by Kane's control of her; and the mother as a figure who acts against her maternal feelings to protect her son from the crude brutality of his father.

While the film provides a critical view of Kane's relationship with the female characters, it does not allow them to develop fully as independent characters: both wives become victims of a kind, as if destined to share in the tragedy of Kane's life.

production history

When Orson Welles arrived at R.K.O., with his special contract allowing him control as producer and director, he brought with him performers from the theatre company Mercury. Thus, *Citizen Kane* was mainly made with actors and actresses making their first moving picture.

Initially, as mentioned before, Welles aimed to make a film version of *Heart of Darkness*. When this idea was abandoned, due to an escalating budget, Welles began work on a thriller. This was also left unfinished as Welles, under increasing pressure to finalise his plans, switched to the idea of *Citizen Kane*.

There has been, as mentioned, considerable debate about who had the original ideas. Herman Mankiewicz, the screenwriter was hired by Welles and then went to a desert motel to do the writing. This arrangement was made to combat Mankiewicz's alcohol problems. John Housemann, who had been Welles's collaborator at Mercury, accompanied Mankiewicz to ensure that his drinking was restricted, and possibly contributed ideas to the script.

Mankiewicz produced a story, called simply 'The American', which would have lasted over four hours as a film. Welles in the meantime, according to his interview with Bogdanovich, had been working on his own version of the script. Later he revised, edited and changed the screenplay produced by Mankiewicz. They worked in collaboration on these changes. The title *Citizen Kane* came from a suggestion by George Schaeffer, the R.K.O. executive.

Shooting began on 1 August, 1940. Having been approached by Gregg Toland, the cinematographer working for Goldwyn, Welles not only employed him but allowed him considerable freedom to experiment with different techniques. This led to the distinctive look of the film. Working alongside Toland, Welles later acknowledged, had allowed him an opportunity to learn a great deal about cinematography.

Toland encouraged Welles to set up single scenes without editing. As noted earlier (see Background: Key Players' Biographies), Toland – due to developments in film technology, including the availability of faster film stock, and more light-efficient lenses made possible by a refined lens coating – was able to overcome obstacles to a deep-focus style. The style also depended on using powerful arc lights.

A recently developed film camera, the Mitchell BNC, allowed greater freedom in camera movement since it involved improvements in sound-proofing. Some shots were taken from below the floor in order to reveal

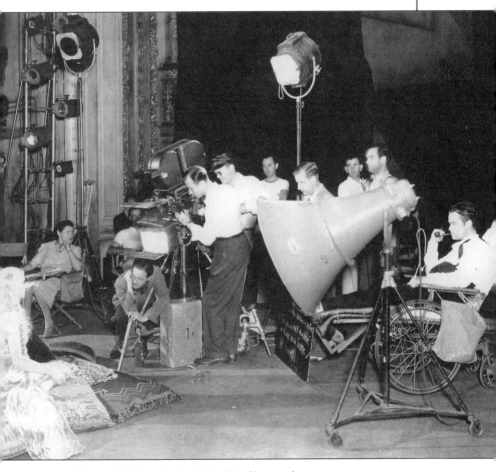

Orson Welles sits back in his director's
chair as a shot showing Susan at the opera
takes place. The prominent role of Greg Toland
as cinematographer (seen just below the camera)
is illustrated as he guides the camerawork

the ceilings which had been included for 'realism', and these low-angle shots gives the film a more distinctive style. Muslin ceilings were used so that sound could be recorded from this vantage point.

Toland provided Welles with crucial advice on lighting and was responsible for an approach in which many of the dissolves were achieved with lighting effects. At the end of a shot the background lights, followed by the foreground, would be faded. The next shot would also be introduced with fades. This approach contrasts with the creation of dissolves through optical processes in post production.

However, special effects achieved in post-production were also important. Linwood Dunn, at R.K.O., worked closely with Welles altering parts of the film and adding new details. These special effects included the lightning flash which obscures the cut as the camera descends into Susan's club; the apparent use of deep focus cinematography when Kane tells Leland that he is sacked; and some of the shots representing Xanadu.

The newsreel sequence was shot in tandem with the rest of the film. Wise and Robson, the editors 'trampled' on the film to achieve the grainy effect found in newsreels. William Alland provided the voice-over.

Herrmann composed the sound-track in twelve weeks which was longer than the norm for Hollywood films at that time. The music was composed while the film was being shot and cut. Many parts of the sound-track were completed in advance of the editing. For instance, for the final sequence the music was 'pre-recorded and played on set, Toland moving his camera to it' (Simon Callow, *Orson Welles: The Road To Xanadu*, p. 527).

The press reported eagerly on the progress of the production, drawing attention to the huge number of sets at R.K.O. They raised expectations of Welles, 'the boy wonder', who tried to maintain secrecy around the production. Welles sought to inspire his actors, driving everyone to seek high standards while overseeing and becoming involved in all areas of the production. He cultivated friendly links with two very prominent film journalists, Louella Parsons and Hedda Hopper. However, he was unable to prevent both women contributing to the campaign against the film.

Louella Parsons worked for Hearst's newspapers and, after negative rumours about the relationship of the production to Hearst, she was

production history

allowed to attend a private screening of the film. Hearst did not see the film at this time, and it is not known whether he ever saw it. However, Mankiewicz had given a copy of the screenplay to Hearst's nephew, who had just married Welles's divorced wife.

It is unclear why Mankiewicz allowed the screenplay to be seen, but he may have acted in this way due to concern that Welles would not acknowledge his role as screenwriter. Action against the film was taken on behalf of Hearst after it had been viewed by Louella Parsons.

Hearst's main source of power came through his newspapers. It is likely that the threat of negative publicity for all Hollywood films, and his personal friendship with Hearst, led Louis Mayer to offer 805,000 dollars if R.K.O. would destroy the film. The offer was refused. For a period, however, it looked as if the studio might desert Welles, leading him to threaten legal action with a view to showing the film independently.

He also sought to publicise *Citizen Kane*, including in this disclaimers about the attack on Hearst. This did not prevent the latter's newspapers providing negative publicity about R.K.O., and excluding their films from coverage. There were also more generalised threats against the Hollywood film industry that were designed to prevent the major studios showing *Citizen Kane* in their cinemas.

These threats even included anti-Semitic statements against Jewish people in Hollywood by people in the Hearst organisation. After a three-month delay the film was eventually released in May 1941 at Radio City Hall, R.K.O.'s luxurious top film theatre. It was, however, subsequently excluded from some cinemas owned by Hollywood studios.

With the limited final release it is not surprising that it was not a box-office success. This was despite great critical interest in the innovative style and controversial subject matter. The film made a loss of 160,000 dollars, although this was recouped later with re-issues.

The lack of initial success can also be explained by the generally conservative style cultivated by Hollywood studios. This meant that audiences may have found the use of flashbacks, and even the subject, relatively inaccessible. Despite being a prestige production, the film had been relatively cheap to produce. According to Kael, its costs

When *Citizen Kane* was first released in
May 1941, advance publicity and sympathetic
reviews drew audiences to the film. But, on a
national scale during 1941, the film achieved
disappointing returns at the box office

CITIZEN KANE Y

amounted to 686,0333 dollars (Pauline Kael, 'Raising Kane' in *The Citizen Kane Book*, p. 5).

Despite Welles's notoriety following his 'War of the Worlds' broadcast, *Citizen Kane* did not fit in smoothly with the basic formulae for box-office success in the US at that time. Although Welles was clearly a 'star', he was not a movie idol in the manner of other male stars used by Hollywood. Neither could the film cash in on an audience-following for an established female star or an established genre.

If R.K.O. had channelled their finances more towards casting known stars rather than allowing Welles such freedom as producer and director, they might have enjoyed greater success at the box office. Ironically, the studio provided Welles with such freedom because, in comparison with other studios, they had not established a secure means of achieving success. R.K.O. turned to Welles as a saviour for their unstable financial situation.

Although the film received an Oscar for its screenplay, by the end of 1941 it was clear that Welles and his team had not achieved the financial success desired by the studio. However, in the 1950s the film's reputation was transformed when it was re-released on television and in art-house cinemas, and received critical attention.

INDUSTRIAL CONTEXT

The mixed fortunes of *Citizen Kane* can be related to the unpredictable and inconsistent fortunes of R.K.O. The tension between Welles's freedom and the studio system is a significant cause of the particular innovations which the film achieved. As we have seen, the film combines daring new ideas and more established approaches to film production. In some respects the studio had a direct impact on the production.

To understand this, we must briefly consider factors in the history of R.K.O., which relate to the film. R.K.O. was the last of the major studios to emerge, arriving in 1928. It came in to being partly because the businessman Joseph Kennedy decided to become involved in the film industry. He joined forces with the Radio Corporation of America which wished to fully exploit its development of equipment for recording sound on film.

difficult period for the studio

Right from the start, the studio was an attempt to profit from the emergence of sound cinema which had started in 1927. Like the other major studios, R.K.O.'s control of production, distribution and exhibition made it powerful enough to achieve dominance over independent companies, and to have influence overseas with continuous co-production in the United Kingdom from 1931.

The studio's power was also increased through the acquisition of Pathe (famous for its newsreels) shortly after the coming of sound.

Despite the emergence of R.K.O., alongside other major studios, with expansion based on the alliance of different financial interests, the 1930s proved a difficult period for the studio. Just as Kane is shown facing the problems of the Depression with the closure of his newspapers, R.K.O. faced various financial crises. In 1933, its financial problems were very acute. Like Fox and Paramount in particular, R.K.O. depended on the ownership of an extensive cinema circuit. The falling cinema attendance during the Depression years hit these companies hard, making them unable to pay the mortgages for their theatres.

There were more frequent changes of organisation at R.K.O. than at other major studios. Another difference was that R.K.O. was not directed in a personal style by a media mogul, but managed instead by a series of executives. In 1934, for instance, David Selznick became executive. Under his control, the studio had some success in attracting talented personnel and made progress towards Selznick's ideal system of production in which producers had considerable artistic freedom.

By 1940 R.K.O. appeared to be recovering from the financial instability of the 1930s. By this point the Rockefellers had become partners in R.K.O., and they had a direct influence on policy at the time *Citizen Kane* was made.

Nelson Rockefeller appointed George Schaeffer who, in turn, appointed Orson Welles with Rockefeller's approval. The fact that Welles was allowed his special contract testifies to R.K.O.'s continuing search for a solution to its financial instability. The conditions of his work at the studio provide a variation on the kind of creative independence that Selznick had started to introduce for producers at R.K.O. in the mid-1930s.

The internal instability of R.K.O. made the practice of working with independent producers a feature of the studio's history. *Citizen Kane* also shows the studio's influence in the importance attached to new technology. R.K.O. had developed a reputation for producing films with emphasis on spectacle, achieved through special effects. *King Kong*, made in 1933, was the most successful film in this respect for the studio.

Since R.K.O. existed as part of an oligopoly, it could not strike out in a completely independent direction. It relied on the other big companies to show *Citizen Kane* in their theatres.

The industry had agreed common standards following various scandals in the 1920s and early 1930s. The Hays Code had been set up as a body ensuring self-censorship in the industry which included a condition that studios should not make films which depict actual living people. However, action was not taken against *Citizen Kane* for the alleged representation of Hearst. One scene in which Kane visits a brothel, following the dancing scene at *The Inquirer*, was eliminated. This related to the Board's concern to avoid any material that might be considered lewd, obscene or indecent. Essentially, therefore, the restricted showing of *Citizen Kane* was based on a campaign of pressure from Hearst's newspapers rather than Hollywood's established system of self-censorship or a legal challenge.

cultural contexts

As already noted, the approach to mise-en-scène shows the influence of expressionism. Expressionist cinema, which is mainly associated with German cinema during the second half of the pre-sound era, was renowned for exploring Gothic subject matter and is recognised as a forerunner of horror films produced by Hollywood. But expressionism also used lighting to extend the audience's awareness of extreme psychological states experienced by the characters.

In this respect film noir, which started to emerge more forcefully as a style in certain films from 1941, was influenced into using expressive lighting to convey powerful moods, such as a generalised sense of urban paranoia, as well as contributing to suspense.

cultural contexts

To provide an alternative to continuity editing, **montage** was often used by the Soviet film-makers in a way that challenged the principles developed by **classical Hollywood**. The juxtaposition of different images or fragments of action was used to create strong messages in relation to the narrative content.

Hollywood film-makers perceived that, to a limited extent, montage could be incorporated within their approach to story-telling. In Hollywood films it is used less for overtly political communication and more as a way of presenting a brief shift in the story to a more general level. A sequence of different newspaper headlines, for instance, which provides a useful and economic way of representing rapid developments in the narrative, is a typical use of montage found in various Hollywood films.

As Bordwell, Staiger and Thompson point out, montage sequences began to appear in Hollywood films in the 1920s and were used early in the sound period for various reasons which included the spectacular effects of the editing itself (David Bordwell in David Bordwell, Janet Staiger, Kristin Thompson, *The Classical Hollywood Cinema*, pp. 73–4).

The newsreel sequence not only provides a version of the March of Time newsreels of the 1930s and early 1940s, but also includes parodic versions of early documentary film with, for instance, the use of a hand-held camera when Kane is shown in a wheelchair.

At a broader level, *Citizen Kane* is influenced by a range of cultural work – the influence of Shakespearean tragedy has already been noted. Other writers on the film have found connections with different cultural texts. Peter Wollen, for instance, draws attention to parallels with American modernist fiction, including the novels of William Faulkner (Peter Wollen in *The Oxford Guide to Film Studies*, p. 27). The fragmentation of the narrative through the flashback structure provides a basic starting point for these comparisons.

Another comparison with literature is suggested by the childhood scene in which Kane is taken away. Here the theme of a child losing his home recalls the nineteenth-century fiction of Charles Dickens whose novels exposed social oppression.

cultural contexts

The emotional quality of Dickens's work showing how the poor and children, in particular, are oppressed, involved melodramatic changes in the narrative. At a very general level, popular cinema as a whole drew on influential writers such as Dickens and approaches to story-telling developed in nineteenth century culture (ranging from the novel to vaudeville).

In using the sledge as an important symbol, *Citizen Kane* relates to the intervention which Dickens and other writers made with their stories of how children can be oppressed and the importance they attached to childhood as a theme.

In Hollywood films children are frequently presented in a sentimental way, but the restriction of Kane's childhood to two scenes and the sledge makes the emphasis on conflict between the child and authority more striking in *Citizen Kane.*

Developments in documentary photo-journalism during the 1930s can be seen as an influence on the film's quest for 'realism'. The freedom to move quickly from one period to another, and for Kane's character to change so dramatically, is achieved in a way that draws on the new approaches to communication developed by the media in general, including radio.

The influence of radio, for example, is evident in the creative use of sound as a linking device between different scenes, sometimes extending to aural 'montage'. Like the press which it portrays, the film glories, at some points, in the speed of modern life. The power to present the public with new information at a rapid rate helped to ensure the expansion of the media during the first half of the twentieth century. *Citizen Kane* tells a story which relates to these developments and provides some commentary on them. The circulation wars between Pulitzer and Hearst are evoked in the competition between *The Inquirer* and *The Chronicle.*

The film seeks to make a distinction between cinema and other media forms. Here, cinema is able to show the press in operation but, through eye-catching aspects of style such as montage, the idea is conveyed that film has a distinctive style of its own. Furthermore the film appears to offer greater access to personal emotions, by revealing the capacity of film narrative to go behind the scenes of stories reported sensationally in the press and more factually in the newsreels, even though the work of these is represented at a fictional level.

The combination of different influences from high culture, popular culture and the media are used deliberately to create a new form of artistic expression. *Citizen Kane* glories in the capacity of film to bring together diverse influences.

FILMOGRAPHY

Gregg Toland's use of deep focus can be seen in various films from the 1930s and 1940s, including famously *Wuthering Heights* and *The Best Years of Our Lives*. An influential director who also used deep-focus style in the 1930s was Jean Renoir. Orson Welles followed *Citizen Kane* by directing *The Magnificent Ambersons*. This also uses deep focus in a striking way and was made with the cinematographer Stanley Cortez.

Subsequent films directed by Welles have, as it has been noted, shown a preoccupation with complex narratives, and tragic central protagonists. Made in 1959, after time spent in Europe, *Touch of Evil* has some similarities with *Citizen Kane* but also involves important differences.

In the latter film, Welles plays a character who falls from a position of acclaim. The fatal flaws in Kane's character (his lack of honesty and lack of fidelity to his wife and child) are echoed by Quinlain's corrupt manipulation of the world around him. Again there is an emphasis on showing the character's personality rather than seeking a full explanation, but in *Touch of Evil* there is even less explanation than in *Citizen Kane* because there is no flashback structure.

In contrast to Kane, Quinlain is a murderer and the title implies that he is evil. This is a film that belongs clearly to an established style of film-making – film noir. It follows some of the conventional aspects of Hollywood thrillers, but stands out because it achieves some originality at the level of style and content. The opening, which involves a strikingly long tracking shot, shows a creative use of film space in conjunction with long take. In this case, however, the camera movement is more extravagant than any found in *Citizen Kane* and the action is used primarily to generate suspense.

Other films directed by Orson Welles include *The Stranger* (1946); *The Lady from Shanghai* (1948); *Macbeth* (1948); *Othello* (1952); *Confidential Report* (1955); *Don Quixote* (1955); *The Trial* (1962); *Chimes at Midnight* (1966); *The Immortal Story* (1968); *F for Fake* (1975).

The commitment to 'realism', championed by among others Toland, and Bazin's writing about *Citizen Kane*, has been developed in diverse directions since 1941. Following the Second World War, film-makers from the Italian neo-realist school put great emphasis on real locations. This can be compared with the importance of background detail in *Citizen Kane*.

There is a shared emphasis on the capacity of film to portray 'reality' in fiction. And new methods are used to achieve authenticity, including the use of non-actors. The Italian director Francesco Rosi transferred the narrative structure of *Citizen Kane* to a different story in *Salvatore Guiliane* (1962) which examines a gangster's life from different perspectives after his death.

GENRE

Genre is used to distinguish films mainly on the basis of subject matter, narrative structure (including characterisation) and style (including, for instance, mise-en-scène and editing).

Citizen Kane does not fit straightforwardly into a particular genre. Genre films provide variations on formulae and conventions used by films within the same genre. In contrast, *Citizen Kane* aims to communicate about the real phenomenon of the tycoon in twentieth-century American history and, as we have seen, has a highly original approach to style.

Also many of the reasons why *Citizen Kane* has been valued are independent of generic influence. Deep focus has been used in different genres. The characterisation in *Citizen Kane* does not immediately fit with character types already established in a particular genre. The film, as already noted, is strongly influenced by the style of expressionism and montage from European film movements in the 1920s.

The tendency in *Citizen Kane* to move away from genre film-making is further evident in the emphasis on fragmentation. Kane's life is told as a series of discrete episodes, which contrasts with Hollywood's overwhelming use of generic conventions to make stories more accessible. However, it has also been shown that a range of Hollywood films involve the mixing of different genres partly as a way of extending a film's appeal to as wide an audience as possible. While the fragmented nature of the narrative in *Citizen Kane* prevents easy identification with one genre, it allows some comparison with a range of different genres.

Bordwell and Thompson draw attention to some of the genres which can be related to *Citizen Kane*. As well as the detective genre, the film can be compared with the tradition of films made in Hollywood about newspapers; the scenes depicting the opera compare with Hollywood musicals; the portrait of Kane's life relates to the **bio-pic**, a genre which became increasingly popular in the 1930s. The distinctive style of the newsreel is also included. As Bordwell and Thompson point out, however:

> *Citizen Kane* is a good example of a film that relies on genre conventions but often thwarts the expectations they arouse.
>
> David Bordwell, Kristin Thompson, Film Art, pp. 72–3

Nevertheless, there are other possibilities for relating the film to genre. Firstly, as we have seen, the film relates to the genre of tragedy. Well-known Hollywood genres could include tragic stories, but the emphasis on happy endings in Hollywood films means that this genre is more closely associated with other forms of culture such as Greek drama and Shakespeare's plays.

Secondly, as we have seen, *Citizen Kane* is in some respects like a film noir. The expressive atmospheric lighting, the pleasure in a complicated narrative developed through flashbacks, and the overall sense of a hostile environment, mean that some comparisons can be made with a well-known film noir such as *Out of the Past*.

In this film the male hero is more sympathetic than Kane, but is haunted by his past. As in *Citizen Kane* the narrative involves parallel action in two

cultural contexts

different time periods. However, given some of the clear differences of *Citizen Kane* from examples of film noir, it is perhaps more accurate to say that *Citizen Kane* may have had an influence on this style of film-making.

Thirdly, *Citizen Kane* – due to the central importance of family conflict, and extreme personal emotions – can be seen as a melodrama. The final third of the film, which explores the strife between Kane and Susan, can be compared with the emphasis that other Hollywood melodramas place on destructive personal relationships.

Melodramas, such as *Stella Dallas* and *Written on the Wind*, for example, illustrate the closeness of melodrama as a genre to tragedy. In these films there is a sense that the leading protagonists are fated to experience a downfall.

In relation to Hollywood films, melodramas have been distinguished in greater detail by the external expression of emotions through the mise-en-scène. As we have seen, the set of Xanadu expresses the absence of love between Kane and Susan as well as Kane's megalomania.

Melodrama is also characterised by the emotional use of music. In *Citizen Kane*, it is used powerfully to evoke a character's inner feelings. For example, Kane's sense of freedom, when playing in the snow, is expressed by the soundtrack which introduces this episode.

SUMMARY

The style of *Citizen Kane* film suggests a strong departure from patterns followed by previous Hollywood genres. However, the film can be related to different generic influences.

One reason why *Citizen Kane* has been so influential may be that it breaks free from the opposition between originality and genre by showing the possibility for a mixture of styles. This eclectic combination of different influences is held together by a narrative structure in which the dominant genres are tragedy and melodrama.

entertainment value

the audience

By the time the film was first released, many members of the audience were probably expecting a ground-breaking controversial film. The release was delayed from February to May and, during this period, newspaper articles and magazines in America drew attention to the controversy surrounding Orson Welles as a new figure in Hollywood.

It is interesting that many of the first reviews do not explicitly discuss the relationship of the film to Hearst. By this stage it was clear that if the film was openly recognised as a satire on the tycoon, legal action might be taken to prevent further screenings.

Analysis of the film has not fully considered whether it appealed specifically to a certain kind of audience.

The initial response of *Picturegoer* magazine in 1941 involved the following positive publicity:

> ... for once the arty film fan and the other fellow who seeks screen entertainment objectively can both have a good time.
>
> *Picturegoer, Vol. 10, No. 521, 17 May 1941*

Audiences were also prepared by the advertising, which included a poster emphasising the entertainment value of the film with the phrase 'It's terrific'; and pictures introducing the idea that this was a film about one man's incredible life.

Bordwell and Thompson draw attention to the way in which the film itself provides the viewer with some clear ways of understanding the story. For instance, they emphasise the function of the newsreel which is used to provide an overview of events within the story (David Bordwell, Kristin Thompson, *Film Art*, p. 77).

This meant that later parts of the film which involve unusually complex narrative and stylistic techniques would have been less likely to baffle an audience accustomed to accessible story-telling. Nevertheless, Bordwell and Thompson acknowledge that the film did subvert many Hollywood conventions. The lack of closure in the narrative and the ambiguity of Kane are just two reasons why the audience may have found the film difficult.

A number of commentators have drawn attention to the way in which *Citizen Kane* appears to demand a more active response from the viewer than most conventional films. Since Kane's life is presented in an episodic fashion, using different narrators, it can be argued that the audience has to piece together the story in a more complex way than is required by most other Hollywood films.

Laura Mulvey draws attention to the way in which the camera-work frequently provides the sense of a detached but active observer of events occurring within the story. This is apparent in the final sequence, as the tracking-shot provides a survey of Kane's possessions from a view that is strikingly independent of what the characters can see. At repeated points in the narrative, Mulvey comments, the viewer's perspective on the story world is made independent from what the characters are looking at (Laura Mulvey, *Citizen Kane*, p. 27).

So, according to Mulvey, the film presents the story as a puzzle which the viewer must piece together (Laura Mulvey, *Citizen Kane*, p. 28).

Available information about audience responses is limited. One impressionistic first-hand account of audience responses to the film ran as follows:

> Audiences hated it at the time because it looked 'freakish' (this writer remembers more walk-outs and demands for refunds at the theatre he was involved with during *Kane*'s first brief run, than any other picture).
>
> *Article by George Turner in Sight and Sound, July 1999*

It is easy to imagine that such a response may have been quite widespread, but we need to remember that the film did finish forty-second in the US box office despite the campaign against it from Hearst's newspapers.

Reactions to the film must also have been affected by the Second World War. In Britain, as in the rest of Europe, war propaganda became an important element in national policy about which films should be made, and film-viewing was enormously affected by this. Also distribution and exhibition of American films in Britain was limited.

Despite this, a 1943 survey by Mass Observation which involved 220 people from a cross-section of the population in Britain who were to asked list their favourite films of that year, involved several references to *Citizen Kane*. The film was only shown as a revival during that year, but a number of male respondents included it as one of their favourite films of the year.

A strong interest in cinema continued through the Second World War, but the adverse circumstances in which *Citizen Kane* was released is one reason why it depended on later specialist discussion by critics for its reputation. Subsequent appreciation has been developed through film education, alongside prolific writing about Orson Welles and the film.

Today most spectators who see the film must be aware of its critical reputation, but are perhaps less aware of how it related to Hearst.

Developments in film technology may also mean that the new techniques involved no longer seem surprising. Deep focus has been absorbed as an accepted aspect of cinema and was followed by further innovations, such as wide screen, aimed at enhanced realism. However, it is still rare for films to involve such a dynamic approach to contrasting foreground and background. This is just one reason why *Citizen Kane* has maintained an appreciative audience.

critical responses

Many of the original reviews of the film included observations about the quality of realism. Critical writing which followed later involved further exploration of this quality. When Andrew Sarris praised *Citizen Kane* in 1955, he sought to show that it was not just about Hearst. He argued that the techniques used by Welles and his team provided a powerful message about American society.

For Sarris, '*Kane* develops two interesting themes: the debasement of the private personality of the public figure, and the crushing weight of materialism. Taken together these two themes comprise the bitter irony of an American success story that ends in futile nostalgia, loneliness and death' (Andrew Sarris, Film Culture Vol. 2, No. 3, 1956, p. 14).

Sarris emphasised how the style brought together 'realism' and 'expressionism'. He argued that the theme of Kane's decline emerged through the screenplay, while the emphasis on 'materialism' mainly results from the images.

Sarris's analysis allows the influence of expressionism to be seen in the use of objects and settings as representations of the loss of humanity which accompanies Kane's accumulation of wealth. He acknowledges that these themes are unfolded within the structure of the mystery story.

Sarris is also known for his defence of the auteur theory. He values the original style and humanistic message which he finds in the film. He clearly relates these qualities to the personal vision of Welles and the other creators behind the film. Nevertheless his argument allows *Citizen Kane* to be placed as an exemplary development of existing traditions from Hollywood and European cinema.

Writing in 1973, Pauline Kael accepts the centrality of expressionism and melodrama in *Citizen Kane*. She recognises Welles's originality, but argues that a true understanding of the film's qualities involves full recognition of Welles's collaboration with others. She places special emphasis on originality achieved through Mankiewicz's screenplay which she relates to comic screen-writing from the 1930s:

> Kane is closer to comedy than tragedy, though so overwrought in style as to be almost Gothic comedy.
>
> Pauline Kael, 'Raising Kane' in The Citizen Kane Book, p. 5

Kael argues that the film is a masterpiece, not because of profound depth but partly because the film fused different styles to provide a completely distinctive form of entertainment: unsentimental, parodic and very sharp as a satire on Hearst. For Kael: '*Citizen Kane* is a popular masterpiece – not in terms of actual popularity but in terms of the ways it gets its laughs and makes its points.'

This critical approach contrasts with many others because the emphasis on a self-conscious style in the film is not related by Kael to a subversion of previous Hollywood film-making, but is instead championed as a pinnacle of the tough, clever screen-writing which Kael values in 1930s Hollywood comedies, such as *It Happened One Night.*

Her analysis was controversial, partly for diminishing Welles's role and partly for providing an interpretation which conflicts with other views on the film which value its mystery and subversion of Hollywood conventions. Welles's point of view was substantially defended, particularly through his interviews with the film-maker Peter Bogdanovich.

Another different perspective is developed in Laura Mulvey's analysis which brings psycho-analytical explanations to the fore. This is a complex approach which requires knowledge about psycho-analytical concepts. Here, I will briefly summarise some of the points made.

Mulvey draws attention to the theme of father/son conflict conveyed most clearly in Kane's relationship with Thatcher. Here, political differences are presented through a relationship which evokes problems within the family for the young male. Kane's problems are related back to the problems faced by the individual male in making a transition from the oedipal scenario of the domestic family into independent adulthood.

As a way of describing Kane's obsession with the accumulation of possessions and Xanadu, Mulvey brings in the concept of 'fetishism', which is used to explain how an individual uses an object to disguise emotional loss (Laura Mulvey, *Citizen Kane*, p. 72).

Following Mulvey's analysis, it can be argued that Kane never really finds a solution to the loss of his mother – a loss which is related by psycho-analysis to a general theory of an original moment of trauma, through Freud's theory of 'the castration complex'. Equally, Kane does not transcend the antagonism to his substitute father.

The problems which stem from these traumas are transferred and repeated in different forms throughout the life depicted. The loss of the mother is echoed in Susan's departure; the conflict with Thatcher is echoed in the confrontations with Gettys and Leland.

Psycho-analytical theory, for instance, shifts analysis of the film away from the emphasis on originality towards elements in the film which can be compared and contrasted with other films from a new critical perspective.

Mulvey relates the film to the political context in which it was made. She draws attention to the way in which Kane's rise with *The Inquirer* can be seen to refer not only to Hearst's early radicalism, but also to a kind of Fascist politics. Fascism involved appealing to the working class and was characterised by the emphasis on power and 'rhetoric'. As Mulvey points out: 'Kane's politics are presented throughout the film as an extension of his newspapers, as inflated rhetoric buoyed up by personal denunciation' (Laura Mulvey, *Citizen Kane*, p. 58).

conclusion

The frequent claim that *Citizen Kane* is the greatest film ever made is obviously a subjective judgement. However, in many respects, the extent of the critical attention which the film has received seems justified.

The critical reputation of *Citizen Kane* has ensured recognition of the film's ground-breaking use of deep focus, the highly unusual use of flashbacks, and other distinctive elements of the film's style such as montage and soundtrack. The film has influenced many other film-makers through these unusual techniques, as well as providing a highly complex example of narrative-based cinema in which ambiguity is allowed a strong presence.

The film's reputation has also ensured continued discussion of its controversial subject matter, and more broadly the whole issue of how we discuss cinema which claims to be fictional while clearly offering material which relates to issues facing the society in which it is produced.

Concentration on the technical achievements of the film should not lead us to underestimate the degree to which *Citizen Kane*'s treatment of power, corruption and alienation continues to resonate into the twenty-first century.

bibliography

general film

Altman, Rick, *Film Genre*,
BFI, 1999
Detailed exploration of film genres

Bordwell, David, *Narration in the Fiction Film*, Routledge, 1985
A detailed study of narrative theory and structures

– – –, Staiger, Janet & Thompson, Kristin, *The Classical Hollywood Cinema: Film Style & Mode of Production to 1960*, Routledge, 1985; pbk 1995
An authoritative study of cinema as institution, it covers film style and production

– – – & Thompson, Kristin, *Film Art*, McGraw-Hill, 4th edn, 1993
An introduction to film aesthetics for the non-specialist

Branson, Gill & Stafford, Roy, *The Media Studies Handbook*, Routledge, 1996

Buckland, Warren, *Teach Yourself Film Studies*, Hodder & Stoughton, 1998
Very accessible, it gives an overview of key areas in film studies

Cook, Pam (ed.), *The Cinema Book*, BFI, 1994

Corrigan, Tim, *A Short Guide To Writing About Film*,
HarperCollins, 1994
What it says: a practical guide for students

Dyer, Richard, *Stars*, BFI, 1979; pbk Indiana University Press, 1998
A good introduction to the star system

Easthope, Antony, *Classical Film Theory*, Longman, 1993
A clear overview of recent writing about film theory

Hayward, Susan, *Key Concepts in Cinema Studies*,
Routledge, 1996

Hill, John & Gibson, Pamela Church (eds), *The Oxford Guide to Film Studies*, Oxford University Press, 1998
Wide-ranging standard guide

Lapsley, Robert & Westlake, Michael, *Film Theory: An Introduction*, Manchester University Press, 1994

Maltby, Richard & Craven, Ian, *Hollywood Cinema*,
Blackwell, 1995
A comprehensive work on the Hollywood industry and its products

Mulvey, Laura, 'Visual Pleasure and Narrative Cinema' (1974), in *Visual and Other Pleasures*,
Indiana University Press, Bloomington, 1989
The classic analysis of 'the look' and 'the male gaze' in Hollywood cinema. Also available in numerous other edited collections

Nelmes, Jill (ed.), *Introduction to Film Studies*,
Routledge, 1996
Deals with several national cinemas and key concepts in film study

Nowell-Smith, Geoffrey (ed.), *The Oxford History of World Cinema*, Oxford University Press, 1996
Hugely detailed and wide-ranging with many features on 'stars'

Thomson, David, *A Biographical Dictionary of the Cinema*, Secker & Warburg, 1975
   Unashamedly driven by personal taste, but often stimulating

Truffaut, François, *Hitchcock*, Simon & Schuster, 1966, rev. edn, Touchstone, 1985
   Landmark extended interview

Turner, Graeme, *Film as Social Practice*, 2nd edn, Routledge, 1993
   Chapter four, 'Film Narrative', discusses structuralist theories of narrative

Wollen, Peter, *Signs and Meaning in the Cinema*, Viking, 1972
   An important study in semiology

Readers should also explore the many relevant websites and journals. *Film Education* and *Sight and Sound* are standard reading.

Valuable websites include:

The Internet Movie Database at
http://uk.imdb.com

Screensite at
http://www.tcf.ua.edu/screensite/contents.html

The Media and Communications Site at the University of Aberystwyth at
http://www.aber.ac.uk/~dgc/welcome.html

There are obviously many other university and studio websites which are worth exploring in relation to film studies.

citizen kane

Bazin, Andre, *Orson Welles: A Critical View*, First Acrobat Books 1991, Venice, First Published in France by Les Editions du Cerf

Bogdanovich, Peter, Welles, Orson and Rosenbaum, Jonathan, *This is Orson Welles*, HarperCollins, 1992

Bordwell, David and Thompson, Kristin, *Film Art: An Introduction*, Third Edition, McGraw-Hill inc, 1979, 1986, 1990
   Includes a sample analysis of *Citizen Kane*, drawing on concepts such as cause and effect and genre

Bordwell, David, Staiger, Janet and Thompson, Kristin, *The Classical Hollywood Cinema: Film Style and Mode of Production to 1960*, Routledge, London, 1985

Bordwell, David, article on *Citizen Kane* in *Film Comment*, Summer 1971

Callow, Simon, *Orson Welles: The Road To Xanadu*, Jonathan Cape, 1995
   A comprehensive and fascinating account of Orson Welles's life and work up to 1942

Cowie, Peter, *The Cinema of Orson Welles*, A.S. Barnes and Co, New York 1973, The Tantivity Press, London, 1978

Gorbman, Claudia, *Unheard Melodies: Narrative Film Music*, Indiana University Press, The British Film Institute, 1987

Kael, Pauline, 'Raising Kane' in *The Citizen Kane Book*, Limelight Editions 1984, New York, first Published by Bantam Books, 1971

Jeromski, Grace (ed.), *International Dictionary of Films and Filmmakers – 4 Writers and Production Artists*, St James Press, 1997

Jewell, Richard B., with Harbin, Vernon, *The R.K.O. Story*, Octopus Books, London, 1982

Leaming, Barbara, *Orson Welles, A Biography*, Weidenfeld and Nicolson, London, 1984

Merryman, Richard, Mank: *The Wit, World and Life of Herman Mankiewicz*, New York, 1978

Mulvey, Laura, *Citizen Kane*, BFI Film Classics, London, 1992

Nelmes, Jill (ed.), *An Introduction to Film Studies*, Routledge, 1996

Nichols, Bill (ed.), *Movies and Methods Vol 2*, University of California Press, 1985
Includes the essay on mise-en-scène in Hollywood family melodramas by Thomas Elsaesser, and also 'Technological and Aesthetic Influences on the development of Deep-Focus Cinematography in the United States' by Patrick Ogle

Nye, R.B. and Morpurgo, J.E., *The Growth of the United States – A History of the United States: 2*, Penguin 1955, 1972, London

Richards, Jeffrey and Sheridan, Dorothy (eds), *Mass Observation at the Movies*, Routledge and Kegan Paul, 1987

Schatz, Thomas, *Hollywood Genres: Formulas, Filmmaking and the Studio System*, New York: Random House, 1981

Steele, Richard W., *Propaganda in an Open Society: The Roosevelt Administration and the Media 1933–1941*, Greenwood Press, Connecticut, London, 1987

Thomson, David, *Rosebud: The Story of Orson Welles*, Little, Brown and Company, US, 1996
An original analysis full of information and critical insights into Orson Welles's life in relation to his films

cinematic terms

auteur the director, when priority is given to his/her influence on the film through critically-acclaimed originality of style and/or original development of distinctive themes

bio-pic a genre in which the narrative provides a biographical portrait

classical Hollywood from approximately 1917–1960, due to a consistent style with a clearly defined approach to film form, Hollywood cinema has been described as classical Hollywood

cutting describes the effect of ending individual shots through editing without the use of fade, wipe, or dissolve

deep focus when foreground and background objects are equally in focus

deep staging an emphasis in the mise-en-scène on details shown at a distance

diagonal composition when the camera is positioned to one side of the action, providing a view which slants across the filmed space

equilibrium a period in the narrative which presents stability, freedom from conflict and disruptive events. The concept was used by Todorov in narrative analysis

flashback a section of the film which presents a period of time prior to that at which the narrative began

identification when the viewer shares the viewpoint and perspective of a character in the film. Also used to describe the process whereby the viewer shares the view-point of the film as a whole

linear narrative when the progression of the story is propelled by clearly defined causes without digressions or complications in the order of the timing

low-key lighting a style of lighting which involves strong contrasts between shadow and light

matte a mask used to cover part of a photographed image, allowing a separately photographed image to be included in the same shot during post production by the special effects department. In other words, a matte shot involves the combination of images shot at different times

montage an approach to editing developed by Russian film-makers after the Revolution. It involves an emphasis on radical juxtaposition of diverse shots as a means of presenting political and historical conflict

realism a style which seeks to convince the viewer that the film is true to life. In fiction film this may be conveyed through pertinent themes and the way the film has been constructed, for example through the use of real locations or non-actors. There is debate about whether different approaches are 'realistic' and if 'realism' is possible

scene a section of the film occurring in one location, and over a distinct period of time, which is not interrupted by cuts to action occurring in other locations or during a different period of time

screenplay this includes dialogue and also the narrative structure and screen directions provided by the scriptwriter

sequence a distinct section of the film, involving more than one scene, but

cinematic terms

united through concentration on a specific aspect of the narrative

themes the main ideas which the film narrative conveys. A theme can be an idea which is developed by different parts of the narrative, or ideas which are given great significance at a specific point in the story as an explanation of narrative events

tracking shot when the camera itself is moved rather than just turning on its axis, which would be a pan

tragedy a story which represents the downfall of a character due to fatal weaknesses of personality. In general, a genre which developed from Greek drama

traits aspects that define a character's personality and motivation, which emerge clearly through the action and dialogue

voice-over verbal narration on the soundtrack where the person speaking is not seen

credits

production
Orson Welles

producer
Orson Welles

director
Orson Welles

screenplay
Herman J. Mankiewicz and
Orson Welles, John Houseman
(uncredited)

cinematographer
Gregg Toland

editor
Mark Robson and Robert Wise

art director
Perry Ferguson

Van Nest Polgase

original music
Bernard Herrmann

additional music
Frederic Chopin
(from 'Sonata No.2')

Gioacchino Rossini
(from 'The Barber of Seville')

Richard Wagner
(from opera 'Tannhauser')

conductor
Bernard Herrmann

costume design
Edward Stevenson

sound
John Aalberg

Bailey Fesler

James G. Stewart

choreographer
Arthur Apell

background paintings
Chesley Bonestell

special effects
Russell A. Cully

Vernon L. Walker

optical effects
Linwood G. Dunn

matte painter
Fitch Fulton

Mario Larrinaga

assistant camera
Eddie Garvin

credits

assistant to Orson Welles

John Houseman

Richard Wilson (I)

special consultant

Russell Metty

associate editor

Mark Robson (I)

make-up artist

Maurice Seiderman

cameraman

Bert Shipman

set decorator

Darrell Silvera

cast

Jedediah Leland/Newsreel Reporter – Joseph Cotten

Susan Alexander – Dorothy Comingmore

Mrs. Kane – Agnes Moorhead

Emily Norton – Ruth Warrick

Boss Jim Gettys – Ray Collins (I)

Herbert Carter/Newsreel Reporter – Erskine Sanford

Bernstein – Everett Sloane

Jerry Thompson/'News on the March' Narrator – William Alland

Raymond – Paul Stewart (I)

Walter P. Thatcher – George Coulouris

Matiste – Fortunio Bonanova

Head Waiter – Gus Schilling

Rawlston – Philip Van Zandt

Reporter – Katherine Trosper

Bertha – George Backus

Kane Senior – Harry Shannon

Kane III – Sonny Bupp

Young Charles Foster Kane – Buddy Swan

Charles Foster Kane – Orson Welles

Other titles in the series

Other titles available in the York Film Notes series:

Title	ISBN
8½ (Otto e mezzo)	0582 40488 6
A bout de souffle	0582 43182 4
Apocalypse Now	0582 43183 2
Battleship Potemkin	0582 40490 8
Blade Runner	0582 43198 0
Casablanca	0582 43200 6
Chinatown	0582 43199 9
Citizen Kane	0582 40493 2
Das Cabinet des Dr Caligari	0582 40494 0
Double Indemnity	0582 43196 4
Dracula	0582 43197 2
Easy Rider	0582 43195 6
Fargo	0582 43193 X
La Haine	0582 43194 8
Lawrence of Arabia	0582 43192 1
Psycho	0582 43191 3
Pulp Fiction	0582 40510 6
Romeo and Juliet	0582 43189 1
Some Like It Hot	0582 40503 3
Stagecoach	0582 43187 5
Taxi Driver	0582 40506 8
The Full Monty	0582 43181 6
The Godfather	0582 43188 3
The Piano	0582 43190 5
The Searchers	0582 40510 6
The Terminator	0582 43186 7
The Third Man	0582 40511 4
Thelma and Louise	0582 43184 0
Unforgiven	0582 43185 9

Also from York Notes

Also available in the **York Notes** range:

York Notes

The ultimate literature guides for GCSE students (or equivalent levels)

York Notes Advanced

Literature guides for A-level and undergraduate students (or equivalent levels)

York Personal Tutors

Personal tutoring on essential GCSE English and Maths topics

Available from good bookshops.
For full details, please visit our website at www.longman-yorknotes.com